# LISTEN
# AND
# LIVE

# LISTEN
# AND
# LIVE

Using the Bible in prayer

## COLIN URQUHART

**HODDER AND STOUGHTON**
LONDON SYDNEY AUCKLAND TORONTO

First printed 1987
Fifth impression 1988

Copyright © 1987 by Colin Urquhart


**British Library Cataloguing in Publication Data**

Urquhart, Colin
    Listen and live: using the Bible in
    prayer. – (Hodder general religious).
    1. Bible – Devotional literature
    I. Title
    242'.5        BS491.5

    ISBN 0 340 41779 X

# CONTENTS

· PART ONE ·

## YOUR FELLOWSHIP WITH GOD

· PART TWO ·

## YOUR LORD AND YOUR GOD

· PART THREE ·

# YOUR LIFE IN CHRIST

· PART FOUR ·

# YOUR LIFE OF FAITH

· PART FIVE ·

# YOUR LIFE IN THE SPIRIT

· PART SIX ·

# YOUR LIFE IN THE KINGDOM

· PART SEVEN ·

# YOUR LIFE OF DISCIPLESHIP

· PART EIGHT ·

# YOUR LIFE IN HOLINESS AND GLORY

# ACKNOWLEDGMENTS

At last! A promise fulfilled! Several years ago I wrote a footnote in my book, *Anything You Ask*, to say that the principles of prayer referred to there would soon be published under the title, *Listen and Live*. Ever since then my office has had continual requests for the book. It has been an embarrassment for me whenever people have asked for the book when speaking with them after public engagements.

So it is with joy and relief that the task has now been accomplished. There have been many causes for delay. My good friend, Alan Woodland, and I co-operated in producing the original series of meditations in duplicated form back in the 1960s. This was reproduced several times, but before publishing them in printed form, I wanted to revise them completely.

The revision has become a complete rewrite, so that this book bears little resemblance to the original meditations, although the general form of prayer is the same.

Both Alan and I would acknowledge our gratitude to the late Jim Wilson and to Robert Coulson for principles learned through their teaching on prayer. I should also like to thank all those prayer groups with whom I have shared this way of praying – at Cheshunt, Letchworth, Luton and more recently in the Bethany Fellowship.

In producing this book I am deeply grateful to the Lord for the love and devotion to the task by my assistant, Angela, and my secretary, Janie. My thanks also to Merion and all the members of my household for their help and encouragement.

Above all, my thanks to our heavenly Father who in love draws us close to Him in prayer and who has given me such a lovely wife, Caroline, to be with me in the service of His kingdom. And, needless to say, my children, Claire, Clive and

Andrea, have exercised their usual patience when Dad has been busy writing, even though he spends so little time at home with them.

To God be all the glory!

The Scriptures quoted are from the New International Version and are used with permission.

# LISTEN AND LIVE

Many Christians want to know the answer to two basic questions:
1. How can I pray more effectively?
2. How can I receive from God the blessings He promises?
This book contains the answers to such questions – a way of praying that has proved to be both powerful and effective over many years. This method is powerful because it shows you how to use the words of Jesus and other Scriptures in prayer. It is effective because God will always honour His own words.

Some people despise methods because they believe prayer should always be spontaneous. Others like a fixed form because they fear spontaneity. This book will be useful to both. An outline is provided in which there is plenty of room for spontaneous expression. You will find the method readily adaptable to your own needs.

At the same time this method of prayer provides a discipline, but not a legalistic form. This is a way in which you can meet with God in prayer, hear His voice and receive powerfully from Him both for yourself and others.

I have used this method of prayer with many groups of church people, besides finding it a great strength in my own spiritual life. The principal benefits I have received through it are these:
1. It has helped me to appreciate that God's words contain Spirit and life.
2. I have learned how to receive that life through His words.
3. Through such prayer it is possible to receive, at any time the love, joy, peace, power, healing, forgiveness, etc., of which Jesus speaks, at any time.
4. God's power and healing can be conveyed to others, by

taking hold of the healing in God's Word and passing this on to others.

5. This prayer has made it much easier for me to hear God's voice.

6. Many Scriptures have become part of me in such a deep way that my thinking and attitudes have been changed by them. In other words, receiving His words in this way can help you to think as God thinks, and to have His attitudes towards your daily circumstances.

When pastoring a local church in Luton, there were as many as eighteen groups using this method of prayer weekly, including three groups among the staff of the general hospital in the parish. These were called prayer and healing groups and numerous people received miraculous healing from God through the prayer ministry of these groups.

In addition one group met to pray weekly for unconverted members of church families and friends with startling results.

Most of us spend only a limited time in prayer, and do not have the capacity to concentrate for longer periods. You will find this method can be as brief or as long as you want it to be, but that it will aid your ability to concentrate.

Some words of advice: It is better not to maintain any other methods while using this one, simply because you will only burden yourself by doing that. Let this become a framework within which you hear from God, pray to Him and praise His name. It is most important that you meet with God in your prayer time – not say a whole series of prayers because this has been your habit.

And give yourself opportunity to become used to this way of praying. It is very simple and will fast cease to become a 'method'. However, at first it may seem clumsy because you are having to remember what comes next. This is why the outline of the method is given on page 17. You will find it helpful to refer to this for a few days until the order becomes familiar.

THE METHOD

This book is divided into a number of short sections for daily use. Each section can be done in about ten minutes, but you can extend this as much as you want. The theme for each section is given in the title.

You may want to use a different section each day, but you will find great benefit from using the same section every day for a week. Not only are you able to absorb the teaching more fully, but the words of Scripture become part of you, when you use them over a period of time. Even though you use the same material each day, the experience will be entirely different on each occasion.

This method can be used individually or by groups. A new section can be used when the group meets, and then used individually by each member of the group until the next meeting a week later, when the next section can be used.

A group meeting does not have to take a whole afternoon or evening. The business of the whole group can be completed within about half an hour.

POSTURE

Different postures are appropriate for different types of prayer. As the main purpose of this method is to receive from God, sitting is the best posture to use. It is easier to receive when you are relaxed; but if you are too relaxed you are likely to fall asleep! So it is best to use a chair with an upright back, but which is comfortable. Discomfort distracts from concentration.

1. *Opening sentence:* This sets the theme for the section and should be read slowly and thoughtfully.

2. *Brief prayer:* Asking the Lord to fill the time of prayer with His presence. Of course, these short prayers may be expanded if you so desire.

3. *Scripture reading:* This is printed in full for your convenience. The New International Version of the Bible has been used. Read this and the teaching given after the passage. To aid concentration you can do this aloud if you wish, even when using the meditation on your own.

4. *Relax:* Sit with your back upright and both feet on the floor. Let all the tension flow from your body by relaxing your muscles. Start with your facial muscles and work down the

body relaxing shoulders, arms, fingers, feet and toes. Remember it is easier to receive when relaxed, and you will concentrate better if you are not distracted by discomfort.

5. *'Come to me . . .'* Jesus said: 'Come to me, all you who are weary and burdened, and I will give you rest' (Matt. 11:28). Pass your burdens over to the Lord. Ask Him to forgive the sins of which you are conscious; give Him the burden of any anxieties or worries you may have. Do all this within about a minute, so that you do not dwell on these issues. Prayer is not sitting down to think about your problems; it is meeting with God.

It does not take long to ask God to forgive you. But be specific. Vague prayers receive vague answers. Specific prayers receive specific answers. You need to know God's forgiveness for your specific sins. Be assured that if you confess your sins to Him, He forgives you; this is His promise.

You are told to cast all your burdens on the Lord. You do not need to go into long explanations. Simply say: 'Lord Jesus, I give you my anxiety about so and so. I ask you to take the burden of this problem. I hand over my concern about that other need.'

Remember, if Jesus bears the burden, you do not have to carry it as well. It is simply a matter of deciding who is going to carry it.

6. *Forgive others:* Jesus emphasised how important it is to forgive others whenever you pray. In this way, no resentment or anger is stored up within you. 'Forgive us our sins as we forgive those who sin against us.'

Forgiveness is not a feeling; it is an act of the will. You choose to forgive. Be sure to forgive all who have hurt or offended you in any way.

Now you are at peace with God and with others. You are ready to receive from Him.

7. *Meditation sentence:* Prayer is an activity of the spirit more than of the mind. You are going to receive the Word of God into your spirit.

Simply repeat the Scripture sentence slowly again and again. Do not try to work out what it means with your mind. God is speaking His Words to your heart. Receive them. They are words spoken from Him to you. You will find it helpful to add your Christian name to the sentence. This helps to make it more personal; God is speaking His Word personally to you: e.g. 'My peace I give you . . . Colin.'

At times it will seem that nothing is happening; at other times you will sense the Lord's presence, you will be excited by the revelation taking place within your heart. You may even be aware of His power pouring into you.

Generally speaking you will have a deep sense of His peace. But do not judge what is happening by feelings. Even when it seems nothing is happening, God can be working very deeply within you.

As you receive His Words in this way, you are receiving the Spirit and life they contain. Jesus is the Word of God and His life can be received through the words of Scripture.

Continue to receive for about two minutes by repeating the meditation sentence. In time the two minutes can be extended to four or five. But do not try to concentrate for too long too quickly. Better a few minutes of concentration than several minutes of wandering thoughts.

Sometimes you can be engaged in conversation and your attention strays from what the other person is saying. In such circumstances you begin to listen again as soon as you are aware your attention has strayed. If your thoughts do wander, do not be either surprised or dismayed. Simply come back to the meditation sentence, knowing God is speaking His Words to you.

As you are receiving the Word in this way, you will find sometimes that the Holy Spirit will bring to mind other Scriptures, or even speak to you prophetically. Do not be surprised by this; receiving His Words sharpens your ability to hear the Lord speaking to you. As you listen to Him through His Word, so you are able to listen to the voice of His Spirit and make use of His gifts.

Two further Scriptures are given which can be used to supplement the meditation sentence. Their use is entirely optional, but you can use one or both of them between repetition of the main sentence, especially when you are praying for longer periods of time. Do not feel you have to use these additional Scriptures, especially at first when you are becoming used to this way of praying.

Jesus warned against vain repetition – the mechanical repetition of prayers which do not come from the heart. To repeat Scriptures in this way is certainly not vain, for you are allowing God to speak His Words to your heart, and you are receiving the truth, life, Spirit and healing that are in those words.

8. *Prayer for others:* Having received the Words yourself, you can now direct them, and the life they contain, towards others. Into the stillness of God's presence bring the person for whom you wish to pray. Continue to use the meditation sentence adding his or her Christian name to the sentence: e.g. 'My peace I give to you . . . John.' You may like to imagine the person is there before you and that you are laying your hands on his head in the name of Jesus, as you communicate the healing and life of His Word to him.

At times the Holy Spirit may prompt you to add a further word of Scripture for a particular individual because this is relevant for the person's situation.

After about half a minute, thank the Lord for what He has done in that person. You may like to use Jesus's words: 'Father, I thank you that you have heard me. I knew that you always hear me' (John 11:41–2). Then pray for the next person.

Try not to have a list of more than about six or eight people. Better to pray effectively for a few than ineffectively for many.

9. *Praise:* Thank the Lord for His love and presence with you and spend a few moments praising Him. You are given a sentence from Scripture to help you do this. Add to this your own words of thanksgiving and praise.

10. *Closing prayer:* This is a prayer of consecration to the Lord, that you may serve Him faithfully and lovingly, taking His presence into your daily life and relationships. You can use the suggested prayer or one of your own.

I have tried to keep the explanation of this method as brief and simple as possible. I have prepared an audio cassette which gives a fuller explanation and which includes an actual time of meditation as a demonstration. You can obtain this by sending £3.00 to:

> Listen and Live,
> Roffey Place Christian Training Centre,
> Faygate, Horsham.
> West Sussex RH12 4SA

May the Lord Jesus bless you richly in your times of prayer. May you meet with Him in His Word and by the power of His Spirit.

C.U.

# PRAYER OUTLINE

1. Opening sentence.
2. Brief prayer.
3. Scripture reading.
4. Relax.
5. 'Come to me, all you who are weary and burdened, and I will give you rest.'
   (a) Confess your sins to the Lord.
   (b) Pass your burdens on to Him.
6. Forgive others.
7. Meditation sentence – repeated several times.
8. Prayer for others – using meditation sentence.
9. Praise.
10. Prayer of consecration: 'Lord I offer myself to you, all that I am, all that I have and all that I do. Work through me by the power of your Holy Spirit that I might please you in all things, and come to the glorious fulfilment of your purposes for me. Amen.'

# PART ONE

# YOUR FELLOWSHIP WITH GOD

# 1. The God of Love

'We love because he first loved us' (1 JOHN 4:19).

Holy Spirit, please show me the love of Jesus.

**READING:** 1 JOHN 4:16–18

God is love. Whoever lives in love lives in God, and God in him. Love is made complete among us so that we will have confidence on the day of judgment, because in this world we are like him. There is no fear in love. But perfect love drives out fear, because fear has to do with punishment. The man who fears is not made perfect in love.

---

'God is love'; this is a truth that needs to become personal revelation for you. Then you will know He loves you personally.

God's love is of a very particular kind; it is given, shared, communicated to others. 'For God so loved the world that he *gave* his one and only Son, that whoever believes in him shall not perish but have eternal life' (John 3:16).

In love He gave His Son for you. In love He wants to give Himself to you now. He loves you so much He wants to live in you in the person of the Holy Spirit. In love He wants to answer your prayers. He wants you to live with a continual awareness of His love, knowing His presence with you always. Instead of dealing with you as you deserve, He is ready to forgive you and to treat you with mercy and graciousness.

The Lord does not look upon you with judgment, criticism or condemnation. He does not accuse you or crush you. It is not His purpose to bruise or hurt you.

In love he wants to encourage you, fill you, provide for you. His love is very practical. He does not sit on His throne, saying, 'I love you', while keeping Himself detached from your needs and circumstances. He wants to be involved in every area of your life. ⟵

His love is not born of emotion and does not depend on feelings; it is born of the Spirit. But it touches the emotions and you need not be afraid of this fact. The Holy Spirit living within you desires to influence each area of your soul, including the emotions. If you love the Lord, you will feel love for Him; but loving Him is not based on feelings. If you love Him you will obey His commandments, regardless of feelings. You will express your love in positive, practical obedience.

Loving the Lord, however, is more than a slavish obedience to His will. It involves a *relationship* of love. When you worship Him it is right to feel love for Him, to feel the joy in praise and the beauty of adoration.

Some try to freeze their feelings out of their Christian lives and that can be dangerous. If you are afraid to feel love for God, you will frequently doubt His love for you. There is no fear in love. The existence of the fear is the very proof of an inadequate grasp of His love.

Allow the love of Jesus to fill your spirit and soul as you receive His Word. Because He loves you, He wants you to receive His love. Know that He is speaking His Words of love to you now; that these are not words about love, but Words of love. They contain His love and communicate His love to you.

---

**Meditation:**
'I HAVE LOVED YOU,' SAYS THE LORD (MAL. 1:2).

Fear not, for I have redeemed you; I have called you by name; you are mine (ISA. 43:1).

You are precious and honoured in my sight, and . . . I love you (ISA. 43:4).

**Praise:**
I love you, O Lord, my strength (PS. 18:1).

# 2. Father

'No-one knows the Son except the Father, and no-one knows the Father except the Son and those to whom the Son chooses to reveal him' (MATT. 11:27).

Lord Jesus, please reveal your Father to me.

**READING:** JOHN 5:17–23
Jesus said to them, 'My Father is always at his work to this very day, and I, too, am working.' For this reason the Jews tried all the harder to kill him; not only was he breaking the Sabbath, but he was even calling God his own Father, making himself equal with God.

Jesus gave them this answer: 'I tell you the truth, the Son can do nothing by himself; he can do only what He sees his Father doing, because whatever the Father does the Son also does. For the Father loves the Son and shows him all he does. Yes, to your amazement he will show him even greater things than these. For just as the Father raises the dead and gives them life, even so the Son gives life to whom he is pleased to give it. Moreover, the Father judges no-one, but has entrusted all judgment to the Son, that all may honour the Son just as they honour the Father. He who does not honour the Son does not honour the Father, who sent him.'

---

God is Holy, Almighty, Righteous, Truth; but, because you believe in Jesus, He is also your Father. Here is the heart of true relationship with God, that you can call Him 'Father' because you know His love for you, that He has accepted you and made you His own.

'The Father loves the Son and has placed everything in his hands' (John 3:35). 'For the Father loves the Son and shows him all he does' (John 5:20). The Father and the Son maintained a perfect unity throughout His humanity because of the love which bound them together. In love, Jesus remained submissive to His Father at all times, even being prepared to go to the cross. Because He loves you as His child He wants to show you all that He does.

Jesus taught the disciples. 'When you pray, say: "Father . . ."' (Luke 11:2). That one word speaks of the relationship we have with the Lord and in which we pray. Like Jesus He wants you to know your unity and fellowship with Him personally.

The Father's love is always reliable. He is the everlasting Father – His love will last for ever. He never stops loving you; He never withdraws His words of promise.

Jesus said, 'My Father is always at his work' (John 5:17). Understand that He is always wanting to work for you, doing for you what you cannot do for yourself, speaking words of faith and strength to your heart, assuring you of His best purposes for you. He wants to draw you closer to Himself, giving you a greater revelation of His love for you.

He does not want you to settle for anything less than His best. In Christian things the good is the enemy of the best. Reach out for God's best. Every human father wants the best for his children; how much more is this true of the perfect love the heavenly Father has for you.

You will find there are times when you need only one word in prayer: 'Father'. Sometimes you will say it in supplication; you cannot find any other words to pray in such a situation. At other times it will be a simple word of adoration: 'Father', the cry of the child to the one who loves him or her.

As you pray now use this one word. You are calling to your heavenly Father; you are embracing Him in love. You are safe and secure in Him. Let Him be your Father; it was His idea long before you had the desire to know Him. And when you pray for others simply hold them in the Father's love.

---

**Meditation:**
'FATHER' (LUKE 11:2).

Father, hallowed be your name (LUKE 11:2).

You are my Son; today I have become your Father
(PS. 2:7).

**Praise:**
He will call out to me, 'You are my Father, my God,
the Rock my Saviour' (PS. 89:26).

# 3. Sons of God

'How great is the love the Father has lavished on us, that we
should be called children of God! And that is what we are! The
reason the world does not know us is that it did not know him'
(1 JOHN 3:1).

Father, thank you for making me your child.

### READING: LUKE 15:25–32
Meanwhile, the older son was in the field. When he
came near the house, he heard music and dancing. So
he called one of the servants and asked him what was
going on. 'Your brother has come,' he replied, 'and
your father has killed the fattened calf because he has
him back safe and sound.'

The older brother became angry and refused to go
in. So his father went out and pleaded with him. But he
answered his father, 'Look! All these years I've been
slaving for you and never disobeyed your orders. Yet
you never gave me even a young goat so I could
celebrate with my friends. But when this son of yours
who has squandered your property with prostitutes
comes home, you kill the fattened calf for him!'

'My son,' the father said, 'you are always with me,
and everything I have is yours. But we had to celebrate
and be glad, because this brother of yours was dead
and is alive again; he was lost and is found.'

God is love; it is His nature to love; it is His nature to give. Because He loves you He wants to give to you.

It is your responsibility to come to Him and ask, believing it is His purpose to give to you. As you move towards God in prayer so He moves towards you in blessing.

Seek **Him** for Himself not simply for His blessings. Desire to draw near to Him because He is your Father and you are His child. You will discover, like the younger son in this parable, that the Father comes to meet you; and even though you feel unworthy in yourself, nevertheless He wants to give to you the very best.

When you receive from Him you can overflow in giving to others. The prodigal son in the parable squandered his inheritance on himself and realised his mistake. The older brother was equally wasteful because he never claimed his inheritance. Like him, it is possible to be full of self-righteousness and pride in the way you serve the Lord and work diligently for Him, without realising you are a son with a rich inheritance.

God does not want you standing outside looking at the feast. As a forgiven sinner, you belong at the table eating the fattened calf, wearing the robe of righteousness Jesus has given you, with a ring on your finger and shoes on your feet! If you are one who has sought to love and serve Him diligently, His word to you is: 'My son you are always with me, and everything I have is yours' (Luke 15:31).

Whether male or female you are a son of God by faith in Christ Jesus because sons have the first right of inheritance, and every born-again child of God has the same inheritance in Christ. God loves you; He has accepted you; He owns you as His child and He wants to give to you.

Receive the truth of His words now. Hear the Father speaking to your heart . . .

---

**Meditation:**
MY SON YOU ARE ALWAYS WITH ME, AND EVERYTHING I HAVE IS YOURS (LUKE 15:31).

You are all sons of God through faith in Christ Jesus
(GAL. 3:26).

Surely they are my people, sons who will not be false
to me (ISA. 63:8).

**Praise:**
My lips will shout for joy when I sing praise to you – I,
whom you have redeemed (PS. 71:23).

# 4. *Forgiven*

'For God so loved the world that he gave his one and only Son,
that whoever believes in him shall not perish but have eternal
life' (JOHN 3:16).

Thank you, Jesus, that you died for me.

### READING: ISAIAH 53:5–6
But he was pierced for our transgressions, he was
crushed for our iniquities; the punishment that
brought us peace was upon him, and by his wounds
we are healed. We all, like sheep, have gone astray,
each of us has turned to his own way; and the Lord has
laid on him the iniquity of us all.

The nature of God's love for us is seen supremely in the cross.
Because He is both holy and just, God could not shrug His
shoulders at our sin and say, 'It doesn't matter'. All have
sinned and fallen short of God's glory. Sin is unholiness;
whatever offends the Lord. The Holy One cannot be united
with the unholy. It was necessary for God to do something to
cleanse us of unholiness so that we might have fellowship with

Him. There was only one alternative: we would die eternally and miss His glory.

Because of our sin we deserve eternal separation from God; we deserve hell, not heaven. We could never earn the right to have fellowship with God. This is a gift of His grace – God giving to those who deserve nothing. So He sent His Son into the world, not that men should be condemned, but saved – from sin and eternal death.

Those who believe in Jesus will not be condemned, but are given the gift of eternal life now. Because He is the Son of God and your Saviour, you need to confess your sins to Him and ask for His forgiveness.

On the cross he offered to the Father His sinless life on your behalf as a sinner; He gave His perfect life for your imperfections, His holy life for your unholiness. God's love is so great for you, He deliberately sent His Son to make such an offering on your behalf: 'For the transgression of my people he was stricken' (Isa. 53:8).

Jesus died the death of a criminal because He was experiencing the punishment you deserve, 'the punishment that brought us peace was upon him' (Isa. 53:5). You do not need to suffer punishment from God for your sins. He will not punish twice for the same offence. If Jesus has borne your punishment, you can be freely forgiven. And when God forgives, He forgets.

Jesus could cry out in triumph on the cross, 'It is finished', or 'It is accomplished'. Everything for our forgiveness and salvation was accomplished. Jesus had made the supreme sacrifice of love that we might be set free.

John tells us plainly: 'If we claim to be without sin, we deceive ourselves and the truth is not in us. If we confess our sins, he is faithful and just and will forgive us our sins and purify us from all unrighteousness. If we claim we have not sinned, we make him out to be a liar and his word has no place in our lives' (1 John 1:8–10).

When God forgives you, He makes you righteous in His sight; you are put right with Him. Rejoice in what Jesus has done for you and know that every time you pray, you can pass all the burdens of your sins on to the Lord. He is willing to take them. He wants to forgive you and He died to make this possible. He wants to see you freed from sin and guilt, rejoicing in His peace. He wants to see you enjoying your relationship with Him as your loving heavenly Father.

**Meditation:**
BUT HE WAS PIERCED FOR OUR TRANS-GRESSIONS, HE WAS CRUSHED FOR OUR INIQUITIES (ISA. 53:5).

For I will forgive their wickedness and will remember their sins no more (JER. 31:34).

In him we have redemption through his blood, the forgiveness of sins (EPH. 1:7).

**Praise:**
'It is finished' (JOHN 19:30).

# 5. *Fellowship with God*

'God, who has called you into fellowship with his Son Jesus Christ our Lord, is faithful' (1 COR. 1:9).

Holy Spirit, please speak the Word to my heart.

**READING:** 1 JOHN 1:2–4
The life appeared; we have seen it and testify to it, and we proclaim to you the eternal life, which was with the Father and has appeared to us. We proclaim to you what we have seen and heard, so that you also may have fellowship with us. And our fellowship is with the Father and with his Son, Jesus Christ. We write this to make our joy complete.

God has made you to live in close fellowship with Him. Fellowship means 'the sharing of life'. Jesus shed His blood on the cross so that you might share in His life and live in harmony with Him.

Many people think that living close to God is something reserved for great men of faith. This is not the case. You can live in constant fellowship with the Father. He wants you to share His life with Him.

Do you really experience this?

It is difficult to be in harmony with God if you disagree with Him! It is possible to argue with Him without intending to do so. If He says one thing and you say the opposite, someone has to be wrong! Every time you complain about the circumstances of your life you are expressing dissatisfaction with God, with His love and care for you. Paul says, 'Do everything without complaining or arguing' (Phil. 2:14).

Every time you think of yourself with self-pity you deny what God says in His Word: You have received everything you need for life and godliness (2 Pet. 1:3); your God will meet every need of yours according to His glorious riches which are yours in Christ Jesus (Phil. 4:19); you have come to fullness of life in Him (Col. 2:9).

If I am living in fellowship with God and not disagreeing with Him, then I know that God will meet every need of mine, not according to my worthiness, but according to His riches in Christ Jesus. So instead of grumbling, the Christian is to recognise the Lord as his provider. Recognise the truth of what Jesus says: 'But seek first his kingdom and his righteousness, and all these things will be given to you as well' (Matt. 6:33).

Instead of disagreeing with God begin to agree with what He says. Receive His Word; hear Him speaking to your heart. Know that the more you agree with Him, the closer will be your fellowship with Him.

As you pray, He is speaking His Word personally to you because He loves you. He wants you to pay close attention to what He is saying.

**Meditation:**
MY SON, PAY ATTENTION TO WHAT I
SAY; LISTEN CLOSELY TO MY WORDS
(PROV. 4:20).

I love those who love me, and those who seek me find
me (PROV. 8:17).

Lay hold of my words with all your heart; keep my
commands and you will live (PROV. 4:4).

**Praise:**
I will sing to the Lord all my life; I will sing praise to
my God as long as I live (PS. 104:33).

# PART TWO

# YOUR LORD
# AND YOUR GOD

# 6. I am your Creator

'Is he not your Father, your Creator, who made you and formed you?' (DEUT. 32:6).

Thank you, Lord, that you have a purpose for me.

**READING:** ROMANS 8:26–30
In the same way, the Spirit helps us in our weakness. We do not know what we ought to pray, but the Spirit himself intercedes for us with groans that words cannot express. And he who searches our hearts knows the mind of the Spirit, because the Spirit intercedes for the saints in accordance with God's will.

And we know that in all things God works for the good of those who love him, who have been called according to his purpose. For those God foreknew he also predestined to be conformed to the likeness of his Son, that he might be the firstborn among many brothers. And those he predestined, he also called; those he called, he also justified; those he justified, he also glorified.

---

Some doubt the existence of God and imagine the world and all life on it has come into being through a series of accidents. This takes no account of the order and pattern in creation, nor does it answer the problem as to how matter came into being in the first place.

Others, even some who would call themselves Christians, believe there is a Creator God, but having brought the world, and ultimately man, into being He then left creation to its own devices. Man has to run the world as best he can, without expecting any supernatural interventions from God.

All this conflicts completely with the Biblical view of God. He created deliberately, not by some chance. He sustains His creation by His Word and everything is moving towards the fulfilment of the purpose He has for His creation. Because He made us with free-will, each individual man or woman can choose to co-operate with the Lord in His purposes, or can refuse to do so.

Within His whole creation, He has a plan and purpose for you. In common with all His beloved children who know Him and love Him, He assures you His purposes are good. '"For I know the plans I have for you," declares the Lord, "plans to prosper you and not to harm you, plans to give you hope and a future"' (Jer. 29:11).

Those who do not know the Lord often accuse Him of being responsible for the devil's activities. The Lord does not desire evil for those He loves. That would be a complete contradiction of His Fatherhood. In His love He plans for your welfare. He has set this hope before you, that He will keep you faithful to the end, that He will raise you up at the last day, that when you see Him face to face you will be like Him. He will not cast you off or leave you to be condemned. In love He has saved you and made you His own.

You are an heir of God and a fellow-heir with Christ. You share in the rich inheritance of God's heavenly kingdom.

Some have placed predestination and free-will in opposition to each other and have said it is impossible to believe in both. The Bible teaches both and holds them together. The Lord has a particular purpose for you, but He works with your co-operation. He wants you to use your free-will to co-operate with Him. He will not force His way into your life, or make you walk in His ways. You can choose to walk in your ways in which there will be no blessing, or in His ways: 'See, I set before you today life and prosperity, death and destruction. For I command you today to love the Lord your God, to walk in his ways, and to keep his commands, decrees and laws; then you will live and increase, and the Lord your God will bless you in the land you are entering to possess' (Deut. 30:15–16).

God has predestined in His love that you should belong to Him, that you should be adopted as His child through Jesus Christ (Eph. 1:5). And yet He waited for your free response to His call. 'In him we were also chosen, having been predestined according to the plan of him who works out everything in conformity with the purpose of his will, in order that we, who were the first to hope in Christ, might be for the praise of his glory' (Eph. 1:11–12). It is His purpose to keep you in His way and He is determined to see His purpose for you fulfilled.

Hear the Lord speaking to you now, giving you assurance that your life is in His hands. He knows you, loves you, cares for you and has a purpose for you. What is more, He will lead you to the fulfilment of His plans for you.

---

**Meditation:**
SURELY, AS I HAVE PLANNED, SO IT WILL BE, AND AS I HAVE PURPOSED, SO IT WILL STAND (ISA. 14:24).

I am the Lord, and there is no other; apart from me there is no God (ISA. 45:5).

For I know the plans I have for you . . . to prosper you and not to harm you, plans to give you hope and a future (JER. 29:11).


**Praise:**
Let them praise the name of the Lord, for he commanded and they were created (PS. 148:5).

# 7.  I am with you

'I have told you these things, so that in me you may have peace. In this world you will have trouble. But take heart! I have overcome the world' (JOHN 16:33).

Lord, please deliver me from all my fears.

**READING:** ISAIAH 43:1–3, 4–7

'Fear not, for I have redeemed you; I have called you by name; you are mine.

'When you pass through the waters, I will be with you; and when you pass through the rivers, they will not sweep over you.

'When you walk through the fire, you will not be burned; the flames will not set you ablaze.

'For I am the Lord, your God, the Holy One of Israel, your Saviour.

'Since you are precious and honoured in my sight, and because I love you, I will give men in exchange for you, and people in exchange for your life.

'Do not be afraid, for I am with you; I will bring your children from the east and gather you from the west.

'I will say to the north, "Give them up!" and to the south, "Do not hold them back."

'Bring my sons from afar and my daughters from the ends of the earth – everyone who is called by my name, whom I created for my glory, whom I formed and made.'

---

Fear is the enemy of faith, and there is no fear in love. Fear is sin because it exists only when we fail to trust in the Lord. There is a good acrostic for fear: False Expectations Appearing Real. The enemy likes to try and plant suggestions in our minds that he knows will encourage fear and which usually prove to be false; the expectation is worse than the deed.

Time and time again the Lord gives His antidote to fear – *Fear not*. That sounds simplistic, but He gives good reasons for our not being afraid.

There is nothing to fear because you belong to Him; He has redeemed you by paying the price for you with His own blood. He has called you by name and He is able to keep all who are His. He promises He will never leave you or forsake you.

The one who has purchased you is the Holy One, your Saviour. He is the Lord whose authority and power far outstrip all who oppose Him. So it does not matter how difficult the circumstances, He promises to preserve those who are His. 'When you pass through the waters, I will be with you; and when you pass through the rivers, they will not sweep over you. When you walk through the fire, you will not be burned; the flames will not set you ablaze' (Isa. 43:2).

When you fear it is because you do not fully appreciate the nature of God's love. The more you believe the reality of His love for you, the less you will fear. You are precious and honoured in His sight and He loves you.

I used to be a very fearful person myself. The more I have grown to appreciate the Lord's love for me, the greater the freedom from fear I have experienced. Even if my first natural reaction to some situations is to be afraid, the Spirit reminds me: 'Do not be afraid, for I am with you' (Isa. 43:5). We are made for the glory of God, not to be creatures bound by fear. Paul reminds Timothy of the nature of the Holy Spirit who lives in us: 'For God did not give us a spirit of timidity, but a spirit of power, of love and of self-discipline' (2 Tim. 1:7).

Is God's love and care for His children not much greater than the love of the best human father towards his children? He sent Jesus to die for us because He wants to gather around Himself the children He loves, those who are precious to Him and honoured in His sight.

How blessed you are to belong to the Lord, to have God as your Father, Jesus as your Saviour, the Holy Spirit living in you. 'But blessed is the man who trusts in the Lord, whose

confidence is in him. He will be like a tree plante(
that sends out its roots by the stream. It does n
heat comes; its leaves are always green. It has n(
year of drought and never fails to bear fruit' (Jer

When the Lord called Gideon, He found him hiding in fear
in a wine-press. Yet He addressed him as a 'mighty warrior'
(Jdg. 6:12). God could see him as the man he would become.
See yourself as God sees you, living in Christ in whom there is
no fear, with the Spirit of power, love and a sound mind living
within you.

The Lord speaks to you now. He tells you not to fear; He has
redeemed you. He has bought you with His blood and you
belong to Him. He has called you by name and chosen you to
be His.

---

**Meditation:**
FEAR NOT, FOR I HAVE REDEEMED
YOU; I HAVE CALLED YOU BY NAME;
YOU ARE MINE (ISA. 43:1).

Do not be afraid, for I am with you (ISA. 43:5).

So do not fear, for I am with you; do not be dismayed,
for I am your God (ISA. 41:10).

**Praise:**
In God I trust, I will not be afraid (PS. 56:4).

# 8. I am your Salvation

'Great is the Lord and most worthy of praise; his greatness no-one can fathom' (PS. 145:3).

Lord Jesus, please give me complete assurance of my salvation through your love.

> **READING:** PSALM 103:1–5
> Praise the Lord, O my soul; all my inmost being, praise his holy name. Praise the Lord, O my soul, and forget not all his benefits. He forgives all my sins and heals all my diseases; he redeems my life from the pit and crowns me with love and compassion. He satisfies my desires with good things so that my youth is renewed like the eagle's.

---

When we consider all that God has done for us in Jesus, we are filled with praise and thanksgiving. We want to bless the Lord, to worship Him and proclaim His greatness.

When you first came into a personal relationship with Jesus Christ, you recognised Him as your Saviour. He wants you to continue to relate to Him as Saviour in your daily experience.

When you focus on the problems you encounter, or the difficult situations which confront you, or the negative feelings within you, the last thing you want to do is to praise the Lord. Sometimes it requires a real act of the will to begin to praise Him. Praising the Lord focuses on Him and away from yourself. Then you begin to see everything in a different light, you gain something of God's perspective on the things that concern you. As a result, faith begins to rise within you and you hear the Holy Spirit witnessing to your heart the relevant promises from God's Word.

The Lord is gracious and compassionate, slow to anger and rich in love. The Lord is good to all; he has compassion on all he has made. All you have made will praise you, O Lord; your saints will extol you. They will tell of the glory of your kingdom and speak of your might, so that all men may know of your mighty acts and the glorious splendour of your kingdom (Ps. 145:8–12).

What a contrast this is to the negative complaints sometimes heard from Christians. As a saint you are the one who is to tell of the glory of God's kingdom and speak of His might. When you complain, you inadvertently suggest that God's salvation and provision for you is somehow incomplete or inadequate.

David knew what it was to suffer opposition, and felt hemmed in by his enemies. He could feel oppressed and discouraged. But he learned the effectiveness of praise. In Psalm 103 he speaks to his own soul as if to say to himself, 'Take your eyes off your problems, David, and remember all that God has done for you: the salvation, the healing and deliverance that is yours through His love and mercy.'

He gives himself five good reasons for praising the Lord:

> He forgives all my sins;
> He heals all my diseases;
> He redeems my life from the pit;
> He crowns me with love and compassion;
> He satisfies my desires with good things.

See how many aspects of salvation are included in those few verses. And this was centuries before the coming of Jesus! Through Him God has blessed you with every spiritual blessing in heavenly places. Praising God for your salvation is the antidote to fear! 'In the time of my favour I heard you, and in the day of salvation I helped you. I tell you, now is the time of God's favour, now is the day of salvation' (2 Cor. 6:2).

Jesus says to you personally that He is your salvation. The Church is not your salvation; your spiritual life is not your salvation; your good works are not your salvation. *He* is your salvation. Trust in Him.

**Meditation:**
I AM YOUR SALVATION (PS. 35:3).

But salvation will last for ever, my righteousness will never fail (ISA. 51:6).

I will not forget you! See, I have engraved you on the palms of my hands (ISA. 49:15–16).

**Praise:**
He alone is my rock and my salvation (PS. 62:6).

# 9. I am the Lord

'Now to him who is able to do immeasurably more than all we ask or imagine, according to his power that is at work within us, to him be glory in the church and in Christ Jesus throughout all generations, for ever and ever! Amen' (EPH. 3:20–1).

Jesus, you are my Lord.

**READING:** JEREMIAH 32:38–41
They will be my people, and I will be their God. I will give them singleness of heart and action, so that they will always fear me for their own good and the good of their children after them. I will make an everlasting covenant with them: I will never stop doing good to them, and I will inspire them to fear me, so that they will never turn away from me. I will rejoice in doing them good and will assuredly plant them in this land with all my heart and soul.

Every day of your life you need to know there is one greater than you, who loves you and who wants to give to you. This God is almighty, for Him nothing is impossible. He is the Lord, the one who is above all He has made, the one with ultimate authority and power.

So great and so personal is His love for you, that He knows your need even before you ask. He is able to do immeasurably more than you could ask, or even imagine Him doing for you. He tells you to:

> Ask and it will be given to you; seek and you will find; knock and the door will be opened to you. For everyone who asks receives; he who seeks finds; and to him who knocks, the door will be opened. Which of you, if his son asks for bread, will give him a stone? Or if he asks for a fish, will give him a snake? If you, then, though you are evil, know how to give good gifts to your children, how much more will your Father in heaven give good gifts to those who ask him! (Matt. 7:7–11).

If God is all-knowing and all-powerful, why should He want us to ask? If His love for us is so perfect, why doesn't He do what we need without asking?

This is the way God has chosen to work, because in asking we are declaring our faith in His love. We are saying He is the almighty God for whom nothing is impossible, and who wants to give to us. Day by day He is the Lord of miracles, whether small or large. This means we expect Him to intervene supernaturally in our affairs in response to our prayers.

Obviously, what you believe is central to your effectiveness in prayer. It is not a question of simply calling Jesus 'Lord', or saying He is almighty, of praying formal prayers ending with the phrase, 'in the name of Jesus'. It is the prayer of the heart that God promises to answer. He will always honour the faith in your heart; He answers what you truly believe. He has committed Himself to do this.

The faith with which you pray depends largely on your understanding of who the Lord is, and therefore of what He is able to do. This is why it is so important to receive revelation of God's Words in your heart. Consider the faith-building truths in the brief passage above:

You are one of God's chosen people;
He is your personal God;
He promises to give you 'singleness of heart and action';
Then you will fear the Lord, you will be in awe of His
    holiness and power;
This will be for your good and for the good of your children;
The Lord has made an everlasting covenant, or binding
    agreement, with you;
Under that covenant He has pledged that He will never stop
    doing good to you;
He will teach you to fear Him so that you will not turn away
    from Him;
He rejoices to do you good;
With all His heart He wants to lead you into your rich
    inheritance.

What a Lord! What a Lord!

You will find it helpful to analyse passages of Scripture like this, and to write down what God says to you about yourself and the wonderful love He has for you.

He wants you to know He is Lord, not only in your head but in your heart. He wants you to believe He is almighty in the circumstances of your life, that nothing is impossible for Him. This is much more than believing in some academic sense that He is the almighty God. Rather it is trusting in His might and power in the daily circumstances of your life. 'Amen! Praise and glory and wisdom and thanks and honour and power and strength be to our God for ever and ever. Amen!' (Rev. 7:12).

Jesus wants to speak to your heart now, assuring you there is nothing too hard for Him to accomplish in your life. Listen to Him.

---

**Meditation:**
I AM THE LORD, THE GOD OF ALL MAN-
KIND: IS ANYTHING TOO HARD FOR
ME? (JER. 32:27).

I am who I am (EXOD. 3:14).

I am the Lord your God (DEUT. 5:6).

**Praise:**
The Lord is near to all who call on him, to all who call on him in truth. He fulfils the desires of those who fear him; he hears their cry and saves them (PS. 145:18–19).

# 10. *I am the Light of the World*

'The Lord is my light and my salvation – whom shall I fear?' (PS. 27:1).

Lord, I want your light to shine through my life.

### READING: JOHN 12:35–6
Then Jesus told them: 'You are going to have the light just a little while longer. Walk while you have the light, before darkness overtakes you. The man who walks in the dark does not know where he is going. Put your trust in the light while you have it, so that you may become sons of light.' When he had finished speaking, Jesus left and hid himself from them.

---

Jesus came as light into the spiritual darkness of the world. 'The true light that gives light to every man was coming into the world' (John 1:9). However, not everybody was prepared to receive the light.

This is the verdict: Light has come into the world, but men loved darkness instead of light because their deeds were evil.

Everyone who does evil hates the light, and will not come into the light for fear that his deeds will be exposed. But whoever lives by the truth comes into the light, so that it may be seen plainly that what he has done has been done through God (John 3:19–21).

John affirms what he heard Jesus teach: 'This is the message we have heard from him and declare to you: God is light; in him there is no darkness at all' (1 John 1:5). We are to walk in the light as the children of light. We are not to be ashamed of our actions or words so that we need to hide them under the cover of darkness.

Sin is often worked in darkness and secretiveness. The Christian can be open about what he does because he wants the light of Jesus to shine through every part of his life.

The Holy Spirit does an ever-deepening work in the believer. On the surface all may appear to be well, but there are areas of darkness, of sin, fear and need, lurking beneath the surface. The value of this kind of prayer in which we receive the life in His Word, is that His truth can penetrate beneath the conscious level of the mind. The Holy Spirit takes the words and speaks them to your spirit, the deepest part of your being. His truth, His life, His light, can then radiate throughout your thinking and can influence your actions for good.

Not only the thinking part of you needs to be converted and brought under the Lordship of Jesus, but every area of your life. The Word and the Spirit flush out the areas of unbelief, of resentment and bitterness, the wrong motives and desires, bringing God's light and wholeness into your life. 'The entrance of your words gives light; it gives understanding to the simple' (Ps. 119:130). This is a continual process.

'Whoever loves his brother lives in the light, and there is nothi    n him to make him stumble' (1 John 2:10). The Lord desire  o cleanse you of everything that is not of love so that you can be full of light and walk as Jesus did.

It is good to have someone who loves you and whom you can trust, with whom you can 'walk in the light', sharing your heart, your problems and needs. This needs to be someone who will not reject you or judge you no matter what you reveal about yourself; but someone who will accept and encourage you, pray for you and stand with you in a unity of faith.

Do not fear to bring what is hidden in the darkness into the light of Christ. You will not find judgment and condemnation awaiting you, but love, grace and mercy, 'for the Lord will be your everlasting light, and your God will be your glory' (Isa. 60:19).

Hear Jesus assuring you that He is the light of life in your life. He will never lead you into darkness. To follow Him is to follow this light and to walk in light. He will lighten the way with His love, joy and peace.

---

**Meditation:**
I AM THE LIGHT OF THE WORLD, WHO-EVER FOLLOWS ME . . . WILL HAVE THE LIGHT OF LIFE (JOHN 8:12).

For the Lord will be your everlasting light, and your God will be your glory (ISA. 60:19).

God is light; in him there is no darkness at all (1 JOHN 1:5).

**Praise:**
You are resplendent with light (PS. 76:4).

# 11. I am the Way, the Truth and the Life

'For as the Father has life in himself, so he has granted the Son to have life in himself' (JOHN 5:26).

Jesus, you are my life.

**READING:** JOHN 14:6–10

Jesus answered, 'I am the way and the truth and the life. No-one comes to the Father except through me. If you really knew me, you would know my Father as well. From now on, you do know him and have seen him.'

Philip said, 'Lord, show us the Father and that will be enough for us.'

Jesus answered: 'Don't you know me, Philip, even after I have been among you such a long time? Anyone who has seen me has seen the Father. How can you say, "Show us the Father"? Don't you believe that I am in the Father, and that the Father is in me? The words I say to you are not just my own. Rather, it is the Father, living in me, who is doing his work.'

---

Some say there are many different ways to God; others that everyone will go to heaven. Both beliefs contradict what Jesus says – and He should know, because He was the man sent from heaven. Nobody, except Jesus, has been born into this world that has come from heaven and knows what it is like there! People only make such statements because they do not understand that God is holy and righteous, and man is sinful by nature. Nobody can be made acceptable to the Father without a Saviour; and Jesus is the only Saviour. He is the only one who has made a holy, righteous, sinless sacrifice of His life to the

Father for our sakes. It is only through Him and His sacrifice on the cross that you or anyone else can come to the Father.

Jesus, then, is the only way to the Father, not simply beyond death, but now.

Many others claim to have truth; but only Jesus makes such a relationship with God possible – and *now*. Only through Jesus is it possible to receive eternal life *now*. Only through Jesus does the Father give the gift of His kingdom *now*. Only through Jesus are people healed and needs met *now*. Heaven and earth will pass away, but the words of Jesus will remain for ever, for they are the words of truth – and the truth is always the truth. It never changes.

Some modern thinkers want to change the words of Jesus to fit their own ideas. They consider the Bible out of date. But their opinions do not lead others to receive new life, the gift of God's kingdom, the power of the Holy Spirit of healing: 'I, the Lord, speak the truth; I declare what is right' (Isa. 45:19). Instead of setting our minds against the truth, we need to bow our hearts and minds before the revelation of God's truth. Then we are able to receive all that Jesus came to give.

The new life within you is the life of Jesus. He gave His life for you that you may receive His life, and only through Him can God's purpose for you be fulfilled.

You have come to the Father through Jesus. He has given you salvation. You can walk in His way, holding fast to His truth, and enjoying the life He alone could give.

---

**Meditation:**
I AM THE WAY AND THE TRUTH AND THE LIFE. NO—ONE COMES TO THE FATHER EXCEPT THROUGH ME (JOHN 14:6).

I give them eternal life, and they shall never perish; no-one can snatch them out of my hand (JOHN 10:28).

I, the Lord, speak the truth; I declare what is right (ISA. 45:19).

**Praise:**
For with you is the fountain of life (PS. 36:9).

# 12. I am the Bread of Life

'Do not work for food that spoils, but for food that endures to eternal life, which the Son of Man will give you. On him God the Father has placed his seal of approval' (JOHN 6:27).

Lord Jesus, please feed me with your words of life.

### READING: JOHN 6:35–40

Then Jesus declared, 'I am the bread of life. He who comes to me will never go hungry, and he who believes in me will never be thirsty. But as I told you, you have seen me and still you do not believe. All that the Father gives me will come to me, and whoever comes to me I will never drive away. For I have come down from heaven not to do my will but to do the will of him who sent me. And this is the will of him who sent me, that I shall lose none of all that he has given me, but raise them up at the last day. For my Father's will is that everyone who looks to the Son and believes in him shall have eternal life, and I will raise him up at the last day.'

Jesus is the bread of life. To feed on His words is to feed on Him. As you receive His words of eternal life, you receive Him. He alone can give you the food that endures for ever.

Jesus will never reject those who respond to His Father's call. When we put our faith in Him, the Father takes us and places us in His Son. He then feeds us with true spiritual food.

He feeds us with the words of life, power and healing. To feed on His words is to feed on Jesus Himself.

Whenever we celebrate Holy Communion, repeating the actions of Jesus at the Last Supper, we proclaim all that His death means and conveys to us. We can enter afresh into the fullness of the life He has made possible, renewing the gift of our lives to Him and allowing Him to renew the gift of Himself to us. Jesus said:

I tell you the truth, unless you eat the flesh of the Son of Man and drink his blood, you have no life in you. Whoever eats my flesh and drinks my blood has eternal life, and I will raise him up at the last day. For my flesh is real food and my blood is real drink. Whoever eats my flesh and drinks my blood remains in me, and I in him. Just as the living Father sent me and I live because of the Father, so the one who feeds on me will live because of me. This is the bread that came down from heaven. Your forefathers ate manna and died, but he who feeds on this bread will live for ever (John 6:53–8).

The Lord wants to feed you with His words of truth, and the Spirit and life contained in those words. He wants you to live in the power of the cross, knowing that in the giving of His body, Jesus made every provision for your physical and material well-being; and in the giving of His blood He has met every spiritual need, cleansing you from sin and breaking every power of the enemy.

Jesus is the bread of your life. Feed on Him whenever you receive Holy Communion. Feed on Him now as you hear Him speaking His Word to you. You will never go hungry or thirsty because of His loving care for you. He will meet every need, whether spiritual or material.

---

**Meditation:**
I AM THE BREAD OF LIFE. HE WHO COMES TO ME WILL NEVER GO HUNGRY, AND HE WHO BELIEVES IN ME WILL NEVER BE THIRSTY (JOHN 6:35).

I am the living bread that came down from heaven (JOHN 6:51).

If anyone hears my voice and opens the door, I will come in and eat with him, and he with me (REV. 3:20).

**Praise:**
The eyes of all look to you, and you give them their food at the proper time. You open your hand and satisfy the desires of every living thing (PS. 145:15–16).

# 13. I am the Good Shepherd

'The sheep listen to his voice. He calls his own sheep by name and leads them out' (JOHN 10:3).

Lord Jesus, you are my shepherd; I want to know your voice and follow you.

**READING:** JOHN 10:14–18
I am the good shepherd; I know my sheep and my sheep know me – just as the Father knows me and I know the Father – and I lay down my life for the sheep. I have other sheep that are not of this sheep pen. I must bring them also. They too will listen to my voice, and there shall be one flock and one shepherd. The reason my Father loves me is that I lay down my life – only to take it up again. No-one takes it from me, but I lay it down of my own accord. I have authority to lay it down and authority to take it up again. This command I received from my Father.

The job of the shepherd is to care for the sheep. In countries like Israel, the shepherd would do this by leading them several miles a day to find sufficient pasture. David said: 'The Lord is my shepherd, I shall lack nothing' (Ps. 23:1). 'He leads me beside quiet waters' (v.2). 'He guides me in paths of righteousness for his name's sake' (v.3).

A good shepherd provides for the needs of his flock by exercising the proper leadership. However, the Lord complained that Israel's shepherds had failed in their calling: 'Should not shepherds take care of the flock? . . . You have not strengthened the weak or healed the sick or bound up the injured. You have not brought back the strays or searched for the lost' (Ezek. 34:2–4).

So the Lord promises that He Himself will shepherd the people: 'I myself will search for my sheep and look after them. I myself will tend my sheep and make them lie down, declares the Sovereign Lord. I will search for the lost and bring back the strays. I will bind up the injured and strengthen the weak' (Ezek. 34:11, 15–16).

Jesus fulfils this prophecy when He comes as the Good Shepherd, who is prepared to lay down His life for the sheep. This is the measure of His love for them. If they are to be led to the rich pasture He desires for them, it is important that they recognise His voice. Sheep, as opposed to goats, are prepared to listen to Him and follow Him.

Those who do not belong to Him do not recognise His voice, nor listen to His words. They are not concerned to follow Him, and so they miss the rich inheritance which belongs to those who love the Lord.

Jesus lays down His life for all – those who follow Him and those who do not. But those who turn to Him in faith are able to benefit from His great love. They know they are loved personally and that the shepherd calls them by name. They belong to Him and are prepared to follow Him. 'My sheep listen to my voice; I know them, and they follow me. I give them eternal life, and they shall never perish; no-one can snatch them out of my Father's hand' (John 10:27–8).

You have the security of knowing that Jesus has called you personally by name. You are His. What was true for David is true for you; so you can say, 'The Lord is my shepherd, I shall lack nothing' (Ps. 23:1).

Hear His words to you; receive them in your heart. Rejoice that Jesus knows you and you know Him, that He has laid His life down for you that you might receive the fullness of His life.

---

**Meditation:**
I AM THE GOOD SHEPHERD; I KNOW MY SHEEP AND MY SHEEP KNOW ME (JOHN 10:14).

My sheep listen to my voice; I know them, and they follow me (JOHN 10:27).

The Lord is my shepherd, I shall lack nothing (PS. 23:1).

**Praise:**
It is God who arms me with strength and makes my way perfect (PS. 18:32).

# 14. I am the Resurrection and the Life

'For as the Father has life in himself, so he has granted the Son to have life in himself' (JOHN 5:26).

Thank you, Father, for your gift of eternal life to me.

**READING:** 1 PETER 1:3–9

Praise be to the God and Father of our Lord Jesus Christ! In His great mercy he has given us new birth into a living hope through the resurrection of Jesus Christ from the dead, and into an inheritance that can never perish, spoil or fade – kept in heaven for you, who through faith are shielded by God's power until the coming of the salvation that is ready to be revealed in the last time. In this you greatly rejoice, though now for a little while you may have had to suffer grief in all kinds of trials. These have come so that your faith – of greater worth than gold, which perishes even though refined by fire – may be proved genuine and may result in praise, glory and honour when Jesus Christ is revealed. Though you have not seen him, you love him; and even though you do not see him now, you believe in him and are filled with an inexpressible and glorious joy, for you are receiving the goal of your faith, the salvation of your souls.

---

When God raised Jesus from the dead, He raised all those who believe in Him. In Christ you are raised to a new victorious life in Jesus. God already sees you sitting in heavenly places in Him. 'And God raised us up with Christ and seated us with him in the heavenly realms in Christ Jesus' (Eph. 2:6).

This is not to say that your physical resurrection has already taken place, but that the Lord wants you to have assurance of your salvation, to know that He sees as already accomplished in eternity, what you do not yet see in time.

The Christian, then, does not need to fear death. He does not know what dying will be like, neither can he experience what lies beyond death until he dies physically. But he does know that death is not the end of his existence, only the threshold to the greater revelation of God and His glory. What he has begun to appropriate now by faith, he will then know fully. The life of the kingdom partially experienced already, will then be fully revealed.

So, like Paul, we can say it is better to go to be with the Lord, but not before God's appointed time. We do not need to fear death or judgment: 'I tell you the truth, whoever hears my word and believes him who sent me has eternal life and will not be condemned; he has crossed over from death to life' (John 5:24).

However, we shall all have to give an account of our stewardship, of how we have used the spiritual and material resources God has made available to us. He does not want us to waste His gifts, but to see our potential realised.

This is accomplished by living in the victory of His cross and resurrection. You are to live in the power you possess as a believer, what Paul describes as, his incomparably great power for us who believe (Eph. 1:19). Fear does not need to dominate your life, because you are a child of God, called to live by faith. 'The life I live in the body, I live by faith in the Son of God, who loved me and gave himself for me' (Gal. 2:20).

Your inheritance can never perish, spoil or fade. It is kept for you in heaven. Your faith is more precious than gold, and the outcome of that faith will be everlasting glory. You can know the victory of faith in your life now, and be assured of the ultimate victory, even over death. You are receiving the goal of your faith, the salvation of your soul.

One of the saddest sights is to see people become elderly without Jesus; to watch people face death with great uncertainty as to what lies beyond. You can be thankful that you will never need to live without Him either in this life or beyond death. You can rejoice that Jesus is your resurrection and life. And you can use the opportunities you have to point others to Him as Saviour and Lord.

Hear Him speak His words of truth to your heart now.

---

**Meditation:**
I AM THE RESURRECTION AND THE LIFE (JOHN 11:25).

Whoever hears my word and believes him who sent me has eternal life (JOHN 5:24).

Whoever eats my flesh and drinks my blood has eternal life, and I will raise him up at the last day (JOHN 6:54).

**Praise:**
To him belongs eternal praise (PS. 111:10).

# PART THREE

# YOUR LIFE IN CHRIST

# 15. See yourself in Christ

'It is because of him that you are in Christ Jesus, who has become for us wisdom from God – that is, our righteousness, holiness and redemption' (1 COR. 1:30).

Holy Spirit, please give me the revelation that I am in Christ.

> **READING:** 1 JOHN 4:13–15
> We know that we live in him and he in us, because he has given us of his Spirit. And we have seen and testify that the Father has sent his Son to be the Saviour of the world. If anyone acknowledges that Jesus is the Son of God, God lives in him and he in God.

---

God has chosen to take hold of your life and place you in Christ Jesus, that you might live in Him. You could never deserve such a privilege, neither could you work your way into such a position. Your heavenly Father has chosen to make you His child and place you in His Son – it is because of Him that you are in Christ Jesus.

You do not have to strive to be placed in Jesus. You are already in Him by God's gracious act. You do not have to attain to some advanced level of spirituality before you can be 'in Christ'. This is where the Father puts you at the beginning of your Christian experience.

He sees you 'in Christ' and He wants you to see yourself 'in Christ'.

How can you know you are in Him? John answers the question: If you believe Jesus is the Son of God, who died on the cross to save you from your sins, this is evidence that God lives in you and you in God. You believe Jesus was not merely a good man, or a great prophet or teacher; He was God in human flesh who gave His life for you – to be your Saviour.

When you submit your life to Him as your Lord, you are born again and God's Spirit comes to live in you. To have received the gift of God's Holy Spirit is the very evidence that He loves you, forgives you, accepts you and that He has made it possible for you to live in Him and for Him to live in you. 'We know that we live in him and he in us, because he has given us of his Spirit' (1 John 4:13).

Every day you are to think of yourself as living in Christ with all His heavenly riches available to you.

When you know you are in Christ you accept Him as your wisdom from God. You cannot have a righteousness of your own before the righteous God; Jesus is your righteousness. God sees you in His beloved Son, clothed with His righteousness, made acceptable and worthy through Him.

He is your holiness and has made you one with the Holy Father. He is your redemption; He has paid the price for you with His own blood that you might belong to His Father eternally.

Because you are in Christ, everything He is and has becomes yours. Hear Him speaking His words to you now.

---

**Meditation:**
IT IS BECAUSE OF HIM THAT YOU ARE IN CHRIST JESUS (1 COR. 1:30).

For in him we live and move and have our being (ACTS 17:28).

For in him you have been enriched in every way (1 COR. 1:5).

**Praise:**
Praise the Lord, O my soul, and forget not all his benefits. He forgives all my sins and heals all my diseases; he redeems my life from the pit and crowns me with love and compassion (PS. 103:2–4).

# 16. Your Inheritance in Christ

'Now if we are children, then we are heirs – heirs of God and co-heirs with Christ' (ROM. 8:17).

Father, may I live in the knowledge of the rich inheritance you have given me in Christ.

> **READING:** EPHESIANS 1:3–6
> Praise be to the God and Father of our Lord Jesus Christ, who has blessed us in the heavenly realms with every spiritual blessing in Christ. For he chose us in him before the creation of the world to be holy and blameless in his sight. In love he predestined us to be adopted as his sons through Jesus Christ, in accordance with his pleasure and will – to the praise of his glorious grace, which he has freely given us in the One he loves.

---

Because you are in Christ Jesus, nothing can separate you from God's love. Jesus says the Father and the Son have come to make their home with you (John 14:23). You live in Him and He lives in you. You have all the resources of heaven available to you: everything that God has given Christ He has given you, because you too are His child and Jesus is your brother.

You received salvation by putting your faith in what Jesus did for you on the cross. You believed in God's grace, that He was willing to bless you although you deserved nothing from Him.

In the same way you learn to appropriate your inheritance in Christ by faith. It is possible to live in Christ without availing yourself of the rich inheritance which is yours through Him. God intends your life in Christ to be a constant reaching up to heaven to take to yourself whatever you need from His riches.

Because you are in Christ He has already given you every blessing heaven has to offer! That does not mean that you have received or appropriated every blessing, but that He has already given them. He has given you in Christ full salvation of body, soul and spirit. So Paul can positively affirm, 'And my God will meet all your needs according to his glorious riches in Christ Jesus' (Phil. 4:19).

You can be confident that all your needs *will* be met because all your needs *have* been met in Jesus. You live in Him who is your sufficiency at all times and in all situations. 'And God is able to make all grace abound to you, so that in all things at all times, having all that you need, you will abound in every good work' (2 Cor. 9:8). Did you know that this is God's purpose for you?

Let the words be personal for *you*. The Father of your Lord Jesus Christ has blessed *you* with every spiritual blessing in Christ. He wants *you* to hear that truth again and again in your heart. Keep saying to yourself: God has blessed me with every spiritual blessing in Christ.

---

**Meditation:**
GOD ... HAS BLESSED US IN THE HEAVENLY REALMS WITH EVERY SPIRI- TUAL BLESSING IN CHRIST (EPH. 1:3).

And my God will meet all your needs according to his glorious riches in Christ Jesus (PHIL. 4:19).

You have been given fulness in Christ (COL. 2:10).

**Praise:**
Now to him who is able to do immeasurably more than all we ask or imagine, according to his power that is at work within us, to him be glory in the church and in Christ Jesus throughout all generations, for ever and ever! Amen (EPH. 3:20-1).

# 17. Appropriate your Inheritance with Confidence

'This is the assurance we have in approaching God: that if we ask anything according to his will, he hears us' (1 JOHN 5:14).

Thank you, Lord, that I can draw near to you with confidence.

**READING:** HEBREWS 10:19–23
Therefore, brothers, since we have confidence to enter the Most Holy Place by the blood of Jesus, by a new and living way opened for us through the curtain, that is, his body, and since we have a great priest over the house of God, let us draw near to God with a sincere heart in full assurance of faith, having our hearts sprinkled to cleanse us from a guilty conscience and having our bodies washed with pure water. Let us hold unswervingly to the hope we profess, for he who promised is faithful.

Suppose someone left you a million pounds in his will, and you knew nothing about this inheritance. Obviously you would not be able to use the money. However, as soon as you were informed about this great inheritance you could begin to draw upon it, to use it in the right way.

God does not give you a million pounds, but a million blessings: every blessing in Christ. Now you can begin to draw on this rich inheritance. If you knew nothing about it before, you certainly do now. As far as God is concerned these blessings have your name on them and He is longing to release them into your life.

Because he knew the Lord, David could say: 'The Lord is my shepherd, I shall lack nothing' (Ps. 23:1).

The Lord is *your* shepherd. He will never lead you into want. He desires to provide for you and meet all your needs, to lead you beside quiet waters, to restore your soul, to guide you in righteous ways. He has spread a table before you in the face of all your problems and difficulties. He wants your cup to overflow because of His anointing on your life. He invites you to take from Him, for He loves to give to you.

Some approach Him tentatively, questioning His love, wondering if He truly wants to give to them. They doubt His love and grace.

You are told to come with confidence into His presence, to come with 'a sincere heart in full assurance of faith'. If you come to Him with confidence you expect to receive from Him what you ask. You do not imagine that you will be turned away empty handed. 'This is the assurance we have in approaching God: that if we ask anything according to his will, he hears us' (1 John 5:14).

Some have been ignorant of their heavenly blessings. Others, through unbelief, have left them deposited in heaven without availing themselves of these riches. The Lord wants you to transfer these blessings into the current account of your experience. His Word will show you what His will is. So when you pray according to His Word you pray according to His will.

Now you can see how important it is to pray His Word; to hear Him, believe Him and confidently ask Him to meet all your needs. 'From the fullness of his grace we have all received one blessing after another' (John 1:16).

Jesus is speaking to you now. He is inviting you to draw near to Him because He loves you and wants to make His holy presence known to you. Hear Him calling you and know you can take His presence into the world around you.

**Meditation:**
DRAW NEAR TO GOD WITH A SINCERE
HEART IN FULL ASSURANCE OF FAITH
(HEB. 10:22).

From the fullness of his grace we have all received one
blessing after another (JOHN 1:16).

Let us then approach the throne of grace with confidence, so that we may receive mercy and find grace
to help us in our time of need (HEB. 4:16).

**Praise:**
Blessed are those who have learned to acclaim you,
who walk in the light of your presence, O Lord (PS.
89:15).

# 18.  Hear and Believe

'I tell you the truth, whoever hears my word and believes him
who sent me has eternal life and will not be condemned; he has
crossed over from death to life' (JOHN 5:24).

Holy Spirit, I need to understand that I have died and that
my life is now hidden with Christ in God. Please speak this
truth to my heart.

### READING: JOHN 5:19–24
Jesus gave them this answer: 'I tell you the truth, the
Son can do nothing by himself; he can only do what he
sees his Father doing, because whatever the Father
does the Son also does. For the Father loves the Son
and shows him all he does. Yes, to your amazement he
will show him even greater things than these. For just

> as the Father raises the dead and gives them life, even so the Son gives life to whom he is pleased to give it. Moreover, the Father judges no-one, but has entrusted all judgment to the Son, that all may honour the Son just as they honour the Father. He who does not honour the Son does not honour the Father, who sent him. 'I tell you the truth, whoever hears my word and believes him who sent me has eternal life and will not be condemned; he has crossed over from death to life.'

Have you received the gift of eternal life? If you have been born again, you have! God has taken you out of the kingdom of darkness where Satan rules and He has brought you into the kingdom of the Son He loves. He has put you into Christ and given you the gift of eternal life.

Paul is clear about when this transference took place: 'And you also were included in Christ when you heard the word of truth, the gospel of your salvation. Having believed, you were marked in him with a seal, the promised Holy Spirit, who is a deposit guaranteeing our inheritance' (Eph. 1:13–14).

This echoes what Jesus Himself taught. Those who hear His words and believe they are spoken from God the Father by His Son, have eternal life. They do not have to fear being condemned, separated from God and cast off from Him. They have passed from darkness to light, from death to life.

The words you believe are the words you live by. You have passed from death to life. You have died to your old life separated from God: 'your life is now hidden with Christ in God' (Col. 3:3). You no longer belong to the darkness; you are a child of light. Satan no longer has any hold or authority over you because Jesus is your Lord. You do not need to fear being condemned; you are a child of God's grace.

Hear these words of truth in your heart, for faith comes from hearing in this way. This is the truth about you, the truth that needs to undergird every part of your life.

Because you are in fellowship with God as your Father, you do not have to act independently of Him, striving in self-effort. Jesus said that the Son can do nothing by Himself, and

He reminded the disciples that they could do nothing apart from Him. The Son gives life to whom He is pleased to give it. He has been pleased to give it to you. He wants you to live in the power of this life and truth, not in independence. 'Let the word of Christ dwell in you richly' (Col. 3:16).

You may find it difficult to understand with your mind, but receive the truth in your spirit. You have died to a life separated from God. Now your life is hidden with Christ in God.

---

### Meditation:
FOR YOU DIED, AND YOUR LIFE IS NOW HIDDEN WITH CHRIST IN GOD (COL. 3:3).

Apart from me you can do nothing (JOHN 15:5).

Now if we died with Christ, we believe that we will also live with him (ROM. 6:8).

### Praise:
Like your name, O God, your praise reaches to the ends of the earth; your right hand is filled with righteousness (PS. 48:10).

# 19. The Truth about Yourself

'Therefore, if anyone is in Christ, he is a new creation; the old has gone, the new has come!' (2 COR. 5:17).

Lord, please help me to know that I am set free from my past and can now live a new life.

**READING:** REVELATION 21:3–5
And I heard a loud voice from the throne saying, 'Now the dwelling of God is with men, and he will live with them. They will be his people, and God himself will be with them and be their God. He will wipe every tear from their eyes. There will be no more death or mourning or crying or pain, for the old order of things has passed away.'
He who was seated on the throne said, 'I am making everything new!'

---

God's Word is truth; that is why it is so important to read His Word, to feed on it and to receive the Spirit, life and truth that are in His Word. Remember, agree with God: agree with what He says about you and about all who are in Christ, even if you do not fully understand what the Scriptures mean. Affirm the truths for yourself.

*Therefore, there is now no condemnation for those who are in Christ Jesus* (Rom. 8:1). I deserved to be condemned, but God by His loving grace has saved me. I do not have to allow the enemy to put me under any feelings of condemnation. God has put me into Christ – and there can be no condemnation in Him! I am not rejected by God; I am accepted by Him!

*Christ is in me so my spirit is alive because of righteousness.* I need no longer consider myself unrighteous because God has made me righteous in His sight. I have Christ as my righteousness because God has put me in Him.

69

*I can walk not according to the flesh but according to the Spirit.* To walk according to the flesh is death. To set my mind on pleasing myself, to dwell on my feelings, doubts and fears is spiritual death. Harmony and fellowship with the Lord are not possible if what I believe and say is hostile to God's Word. To set my mind on the Spirit, who declares God's Word to me – that is life and peace.

*I can live in the Spirit, not in the flesh, because the Spirit of God dwells in me.* What belongs to my old nature no longer need control my life. Because the old is dead I do not have to fight it. I reckon it as dead. God wants me to believe and declare that I am a new creature in Christ. I am a new creation.

*I am led by the Spirit of God because I am a son of God.* Since His Spirit is leading me, I can walk in the confidence and assurance that He will lead me in the path that He wants. If I start diverging from His way I shall soon lose my peace because my fellowship with Him is marred.

*I did not receive the spirit of slavery to fall back into fear, but I have received the spirit of sonship. Every time I say 'Abba' 'Father' it is the Spirit Himself bearing witness with my spirit that I am a child of God. If I am His child then I am an heir of God and a fellow-heir with Christ* (See Rom. 8:15). I am a child of God. He is my Father. The Holy Spirit within me bears witness to this truth. As a child of God I am a fellow-heir with Christ.

Notice the way in which the truths of Scripture are personally appropriated. I see myself as God sees me and speak to myself as He speaks of me in His Word. These same truths are true for you. As you learn to be still and to receive from God you will find His Words will become part of your thinking and believing.

Hear the Spirit taking the truth of God's Word and declaring it to you now. You are a new creation. The old has gone in your life and the new *has* come. Hear Him and believe Him.

---

**Meditation:**
THEREFORE, IF ANYONE IS IN CHRIST, HE IS A NEW CREATION; THE OLD HAS GONE, THE NEW HAS COME! (2 COR. 5:17).

I am making everything new (REV. 21:5).

Put on the new self, created to be like God in true righteousness and holiness (EPH. 4:24).

**Praise:**
For you make me glad by your deeds, O Lord; I sing for joy at the works of your hands (PS. 92:4).

# 20. *Confession of Faith*

'Put away perversity from your mouth; keep corrupt talk far from your lips' (PROV. 4:24).

Holy Spirit, give me the grace to speak the truths of your word about myself.

### READING: PROVERBS 4:20–7
My son, pay attention to what I say; listen closely to my words. Do not let them out of your sight, keep them within your heart; for they are life to those who find them and health to a man's whole body. Above all else, guard your heart, for it is the wellspring of life. Put away perversity from your mouth; keep corrupt talk far from your lips. Let your eyes look straight ahead, fix your gaze directly before you. Make level paths for your feet and take only ways that are firm. Do not swerve to the right or the left; keep your foot from evil.

In order to fight the good fight of faith, we need to 'confess' – to speak out – our faith. We are not only to 'confess' sins, but to 'confess' faith. For example, when we speak as if we were still living in the old life, rather than in the new life given us in Christ, we deny the very Spirit of God within us. Many Christians wage war against the old life and experience defeat because they are fighting a battle already won.

They need to realise they have died to the old life and need live in it no longer. Now they can live the new life, because they are not in bondage to the past. Believing the revelation of Scripture means they can see the power of God expressed in their lives far more freely. They can experience for themselves the victory He has already won.

Such a confession would say:

Father I have failed you. I'm sorry and I ask you to forgive me. I thank you that you have forgiven me because your Word says: 'If we confess our sins he is faithful and just and will forgive us our sins and purify us from all unrighteousness' (1 John 1:9). I believe you have forgiven me, Father, that I am righteous in your sight because you have cleansed me from all unrighteousness by the blood of Jesus. I confess that you are my Father and I am your child; and that you have given me your Spirit. I confess that you live in me by the power of your Spirit. I confess that you have made me an heir with Christ of all you have to give. I confess, Father, that every spiritual blessing in the heavenly realms is already mine. I confess, Father, that according to your Word I am more than a conqueror. I confess that according to your Word you always lead me in triumph. I confess that according to your Word you have not given me a spirit of fear, but of power and love and a sound mind. I confess that I am already justified, sanctified and glorified, not by what I have done but by what you have done for me in Christ; I am accepted, made holy and seated in heavenly places in Christ. I confess that although of myself I was unworthy, you have made me worthy by the blood of Jesus.

When you make such a confession as this, you agree with God concerning what He says about you. Holding fast to the truth will enable you to overcome temptation, fear and a sense of total inadequacy. When you think of yourself as God thinks, this has practical consequences for you. Of course He is wanting you to live up to your high calling in Christ. Even when you fail to do so, He is ready to restore you as soon as you turn to Him in repentance. What love!

In love He has called and chosen you to be His child. In love He has incorporated you into Christ. In love He has given you a rich inheritance. When you live in Him you live in the one who is love.

Lister. to Him speak His words of love to you now. Jesus is telling you that He loves you in the same way the Father loved Him. What a glorious truth! He tells you to live in that truth, to remain in His love.

---

**Meditation:**
I HAVE PUT MY WORDS IN YOUR MOUTH (JER. 1:9).

I open my lips to speak what is right (PROV. 8:6).

My mouth speaks what is true (PROV. 8:7).

**Praise:**
May the words of my mouth and the meditation of my heart be pleasing in your sight, O Lord, my Rock and my Redeemer (PS. 19:14).

# 21. Feelings or Truth

'Heaven and earth will pass away, but my words will never pass away' (MATT. 24:35).

Lord, I do not want to live by my feelings, but by your truth.

> **READING:** JOHN 8:31–2, 36
> To the Jews who had believed him, Jesus said, 'If you hold to my teaching, you are really my disciples. Then you will know the truth, and the truth will set you free. . . So if the Son sets you free, you will be free indeed.'

---

When your feelings contradict what God says in His Word, both cannot be right!

Feelings are totally unreliable because they change so rapidly as you react to what goes on around you. You can feel great one moment, only to feel completely deflated the next because someone has said something unloving or critical to you, or because you have received bad news.

Many live in bondage to their feelings. They do what they feel like doing, and refuse to do what they do not want to do. Satan feeds negative things in people's minds in an attempt to make them feel oppressed or depressed. Even good feelings can do great harm leading to much of the permissive thinking so prevalent today: 'If it feels good, do it!'

God wants to teach you how to live in fellowship with Him, to agree with Him – and not allow your feelings to control you. If you speak only as you feel, you will often contradict what God says about you. In which case you cannot then be speaking the truth. God is truth; His words are truth. Therefore, whatever disagrees with Him cannot be truth. Anyone denying the Word of God cannot be speaking the truth.

Some say, 'I can't deny my feelings, it would be unreal to do so.' God is asking you to control your feelings and not to let them control you. Let the Word of God determine the course of your life, not your feelings which fluctuate so easily. You can be in bondage to your feelings, or be set free by the truth.

Heaven and earth will pass away, but my words will never pass away (Matt. 24:35).
. . . the word of our God stands for ever (Isa. 40:8).
(My words) are life to those who find them and health to a man's whole body (Prov. 4:22).
The words I have spoken to you are spirit and they are life (John 6:63).

Believe the power and authority of God's Word to be the ultimate truth, not your feelings, nor your circumstances, nor the lies of Satan, nor the opinions of men, nor your own understanding of events. None of these is to be trusted. But God's Word is trustworthy and the Holy Spirit wants to speak those words to your heart.

This is where the role of the Spirit and the Word come together. Jesus Christ said that the Holy Spirit will guide you into all truth (John 16:13). 'The Spirit will take from what is mine and make it known to you' (John 16:15). Your feelings will often lead you into trouble; the truth will set you free. Then you will have a greater control over your feelings; they will come under the ruling of the Holy Spirit.

Every time you pray in this way, you are able to receive the Spirit and life that are in God's Word. Know He is renewing His gifts to you now; He is breathing His Spirit and life into you as you pray.

---

**Meditation:**
THE WORDS I HAVE SPOKEN TO YOU ARE SPIRIT AND THEY ARE LIFE (JOHN 6:63).

The Spirit will take from what is mine and make it known to you (JOHN 16:15).

**Praise:**
Praise the Lord, O my soul; all my inmost being,
praise his holy name (PS. 103:1).

# 22. *Freedom in Christ*

'It is for freedom that Christ has set us free' (GAL. 5:1).

Father, I want to live in the freedom you have given me
through Jesus.

### READING: GALATIANS 5:1, 13
It is for freedom that Christ has set us free. Stand firm,
then, and do not let yourselves be burdened again by a
yoke of slavery . . . You, my brothers, were called to
be free. But do not use your freedom to indulge the
sinful nature; rather, serve one another in love.

Paul speaks of 'the glorious freedom of the children of God'
(Rom. 8:21). God wants you to be free. Jesus died to set you
free. What He has done, He has done. It is finished, accomplished. *He has set you free.* And Jesus Himself said: 'So if the
Son sets you free, you will be free indeed' (John 8:36).

Speak this truth to yourself about yourself: Christ has set *me*
free. Christ *has* set me free. Christ has set me *free.* He has done
it. The Spirit of God bears witness to the truth of God's Word.
I am set free through Jesus Christ. I have the glorious freedom
of the children of God. Hallelujah!

Some believe this and live in freedom; others doubt it and
live in bondage. This freedom needs to be expressed in every
area of your life. Some feel there are certain things that restrict
or inhibit them. Often they point to events in the past, or the
way they were brought up. They claim they cannot be free
now because they are victims of their past.

But Christ has done everything to set you free. Because you

76

are born again the old has passed away and the new has come. The only hurts from the past that continue to have influence in your life are those you have not forgiven. If someone hurts you and you forgive him or her, that is the end of the matter. But if you do not forgive, the bitterness, resentment and anger seethe deep within you making the wound worse. Resentment is like a spiritual cancer eating away inside a person. You can become a hurt or wounded person who expects to be rejected and hurt further by others, if you do not forgive.

Do not allow any such hurt to rob you of your freedom in Christ. Forgive any who have hurt you; pray for them; and invite the Holy Spirit to come into the wounded areas of your life. Know that Jesus frees you in those areas; He was wounded to free you from all your wounds. The truth of what Jesus has done for you sets you free.

Live in His words of truth and rejoice in the freedom He has given you. Hear Him speaking His Words to you now.

---

### Meditation:
IF THE SON SETS YOU FREE, YOU WILL BE FREE INDEED (JOHN 8:36).

It is for freedom that Christ has set us free (GAL. 5:1).

In my anguish I cried to the Lord, and he answered by setting me free (PS. 118:5).

### Praise:
You are my God, and I will give thanks; you are my God, and I will exalt you (PS. 118:28).

# 23. No Condemnation

'Therefore, there is now no condemnation for those who are in Christ Jesus' (ROM. 8:1).

Thank you, Father, that there is no condemnation for me.

### READING: JOHN 3:16–18
For God so loved the world that he gave his one and only Son, that whoever believes in him shall not perish but have eternal life. For God did not send his Son into the world to condemn the world, but to save the world through him. Whoever believes in him is not condemned, but whoever does not believe stands condemned already because he has not believed in the name of God's one and only Son.

---

You are in Christ Jesus. You are part of God's kingdom. You live in Him and He lives in you. One of the most important consequences which arises from these truths is that there is no condemnation for you.

Before you came to faith in Jesus you were under condemnation: 'Whoever believes in him is not condemned, but whoever does not believe stands condemned already because he has not believed in the name of God's one and only Son' (John 3:18). When you became a believer, God took hold of your life and placed you 'in Christ Jesus'. He rescued you from the dominion of darkness and brought you into the kingdom of the Son He loves.

In Christ there can be no condemnation, no sentence of death, no alienation from God. Outside of Him all are condemned because of their unbelief; they remain in darkness, subject to the prince of darkness.

Jesus has rescued you from condemnation and there is nothing Satan can do about that. He cannot undo what God has done in your life, but he can try to prevent you from living in the good of it. And one of his chief weapons is to create a false sense of condemnation.

Jesus died on the cross to free you from the shame and guilt of sin and from all condemnation. He suffered the punishment you deserve so you may be spared from punishment.

But Satan wants you to believe you are not truly forgiven, not really accepted by God. He feeds negative thoughts to you suggesting you are too unworthy to receive anything from the Lord. He questions whether God truly loves you; if so, why does He allow difficulties in your life? He suggests you are a spiritual failure and delights to point out all your blemishes to you, trying to make you feel you could not expect to receive blessing from the Lord.

He persists with his slanderous accusations trying to drive us into feelings of failure, frustration, defeat and even despair.

But God's Word here proclaims a great truth to our hearts. There is no condemnation for those in Christ. You are not condemned; you are forgiven and accepted. You do not have to listen to the enemy's lies. Even when you sin, God does not condemn you. He does not throw you out of His kingdom or withdraw your inheritance from you. He convicts you of your sin through the Holy Spirit working in you, drawing you to repentance and back into unity with Him and His purposes.

Conviction, the Holy Spirit pointing out your sin to draw you to repentance and forgiveness, leads to freedom; condemnation is like a prison. God has freed you from the prison of unbelief and condemnation. Resist the lies of the enemy and he will have to flee from you. As you live out your life in Christ Jesus there never will be any condemnation in this life or beyond. Alleluia!

Hear the words in your heart now. There is no condemnation for you because you are in Christ.

---

**Meditation:**
THEREFORE, THERE IS NOW NO CONDEMNATION FOR THOSE WHO ARE IN CHRIST JESUS (ROM. 8:1).

Whoever believes in him [Jesus] is not condemned (JOHN 3:18).

The prince of this world [Satan] now stands condemned (JOHN 16:11).

**Praise:**
The Lord is compassionate and gracious, slow to anger, abounding in love (PS. 103:8).

# 24. *The Truth in Love*

'You, therefore, have no excuse, you who pass judgment on someone else, for at whatever point you judge the other, you are condemning yourself, because you who pass judgment do the same things' (ROM. 2:1).

Please, Father, help me by your Holy Spirit not to judge and condemn others.

### READING: COLOSSIANS 3:12–14
Therefore, as God's chosen people, holy and dearly loved, clothe yourselves with compassion, kindness, humility, gentleness and patience. Bear with each other and forgive whatever grievances you may have against one another. Forgive as the Lord forgave you. And over all these virtues put on love, which binds them all together in perfect unity.

Condemnation does not only come directly from the enemy. Believing the negative things others say to you can bring a sense of condemnation. People gossip, criticise and condemn. Jesus said, 'Do not judge, or you too will be judged. For in the same way you judge others, you will be judged, and with the measure you use, it will be measured to you' (Matt. 7:1–2).

Judging others is completely the opposite to the forgiving, accepting and loving way in which God deals with us. He could judge us but chooses not to.

Satan is the accuser of the brethren, but he can use the mouths of others to do his accusing work for him. Many of the things others say are a denial of the truth about who you are in Christ. It is so easy to listen to, and believe, these negative things, especially if you have a low opinion of yourself already. The negative suggestions and criticisms of others will only confirm what you already believe about yourself, adding to your sense of personal failure.

When the woman caught in the act of adultery was brought before Jesus, He said: 'If any one of you is without sin, let him be the first to throw a stone at her' (John 8:7). One by one the crowd left until Jesus was alone with the woman. 'Has no-one condemned you?' He asked her. When she answered, 'No-one sir,' 'Then neither do I condemn you,' Jesus declared. 'Go now and leave your life of sin' (vv.10–11).

Many people criticise and condemn others because they are so insecure themselves. If they can make others seem worse, this will build their own self-confidence and pride, they imagine. In fact, it only adds to their insecurity for the reasons Jesus gives. You receive back from others what you give to others.

This does not mean that we should close our ears to helpful and objective criticism. Listen to those who are productive in the Lord. Often you will find that those who condemn, produce little themselves. Always assess what people say against the revelation of Scripture, and do not listen to the wild accusations of a single voice. If criticism is valid there will be at least two or three witnesses of the same mind.

To speak the truth in love to someone means that you will point them to the positive truth of what God has done for them in Christ; you are seeking to encourage them, not to be negative and destructive. Speak always in love, and only correct others when you know you do so in genuine love.

The truth brings conviction of sin, but never condemnation. There is *no* condemnation for those who are in Christ – no condemnation either from Satan or others.

Don't allow others to condemn you, and avoid feeding condemning thoughts to others. Know the Lord is merciful and gracious and wants to express those qualities through you to others.

Hear the Lord speaking to you now, knowing the Holy Spirit will help you to fulfil His words.

---

**Meditation:**
DO NOT JUDGE, AND YOU WILL NOT BE JUDGED. DO NOT CONDEMN, AND YOU WILL NOT BE CONDEMNED. FORGIVE, AND YOU WILL BE FORGIVEN (LUKE 6:37).

Then neither do I condemn you (JOHN 8:11).

Therefore, let us stop passing judgment on one another (ROM. 14:13).

**Praise:**
In God, whose word I praise, in the Lord, whose word I praise – in God I trust; I will not be afraid. What can man do to me? (PS. 56:10–11).

# 25. A False Cage

'Ask and it will be given to you' (LUKE 11:9).

Holy Spirit, help me to be faithful by being positive in my attitudes.

**READING: PHILIPPIANS 4:4–7**
Rejoice in the Lord always. I will say it again: Rejoice! Let your gentleness be evident to all. The Lord is near. Do not be anxious about anything, but in everything, by prayer and petition, with thanksgiving, present your requests to God. And the peace of God, which transcends all understanding, will guard your hearts and your minds in Christ Jesus.

---

We can create cages for ourselves by our words, making ourselves feel condemned. Unbelief is like a prison and is often evident by the things we say. Although there is no condemnation for those who are in Christ, we can feel condemned when guilty of negative unbelief, saying such things as:

'I don't believe it is God's will to heal me'; or
'God wouldn't be concerned about this matter'; or
'I don't want to bother God with my need'; or
'There are many far worse off than I am'.

By words such as these we both limit God and argue with Him, for His Word says He is almighty and for Him nothing is impossible. Never question His love and concern, nor doubt His graciousness. You will not see God do anything about your situation while you do not believe that He will. Jesus tells you to ask and promises you will receive, for He is always ready to be merciful to you.

Paul reinforces Jesus's words. He tells you not to be anxious about *anything*. You can entrust every situation to the Lord, no matter how large or seemingly insignificant. In *everything* you are to present your requests to God. Everything means everything!

Some say they do not want to ask anything for themselves. This is not humility; it is rank disobedience to God's Word and is also evidence of unbelief. Only a fool would fail to ask God to meet his need if he believed the answer was only a prayer away.

When you pray and present your petitions to God, you can do so with thanksgiving, confident that He hears and answers you. This is the kind of faith the Lord wants to produce in you.

It is a natural reaction to become anxious about difficult circumstances, but you are told to cast all your anxiety on the Lord for He cares for you. This is why at the beginning of your time of meditation it is so important to spend a few moments passing your burdens on to Him – not spending time dwelling upon them, but recognising that He is willing to take the weight of them from you.

'Come to me, all you who are weary and burdened, and I will give you rest' (Matt. 11:28). Anxiety never helps and is a contradiction to faith in Jesus. He is the Lord who loves you and wants to carry the weight of any problem and give you rest. To know He is willing to undertake for you enables the peace of Jesus to fill your heart and mind.

To pray with thanksgiving is evidence that you believe God has heard you and answered, even before there is anything to show for such faith. Such thanksgiving demonstrates a confidence in the gracious love and faithfulness of the Lord. To pray with thanksgiving and to speak with positive faith demonstrates that you refuse to be imprisoned in a false cage of unbelief. You will not condemn yourself with negative thinking.

---

**Meditation:**
ASK AND YOU WILL RECEIVE, AND YOUR JOY WILL BE COMPLETE (JOHN 16:24).

in everything, by prayer and petition, with thanksgiving, present your requests to God (PHIL. 4:6).

And the peace of God, which transcends all understanding, will guard your hearts and your minds in Christ Jesus (PHIL. 4:7).

**Praise:**
I sought the Lord, and he answered me; he delivered me from all my fears. Those who look to him are radiant; their faces are never covered with shame (PS. 34:4–5).

# 26. *Encourage Others*

'Whoever loves his brother lives in the light, and there is nothing in him to make him stumble' (1 JOHN 2:10).

Holy Spirit, help me to encourage others.

### READING: COLOSSIANS 3:15–17
Let the peace of Christ rule in your hearts, since as members of one body you were called to peace. And be thankful. Let the word of Christ dwell in you richly as you teach and admonish one another with all wisdom, and as you sing psalms, hymns and spiritual songs with gratitude in your hearts to God. And whatever you do, whether in word or deed, do it all in the name of the Lord Jesus, giving thanks to God the Father through him.

We have a great responsibility to build up one another in love, to encourage one another in truth. When Christians criticise and judge each other they only glorify the accuser of the brethren. We need to eradicate destructive criticism and begin to encourage faith in the Word.

This needs to be done sensitively – the Word spoken in the power of the Spirit encourages faith. Jesus intends you to have a ministry of encouragement to your brothers and sisters. The Word spoken without love can leave people feeling devastated even if what is said is true. It is not only what you say that matters but how you say it! You need to speak the truth in love, and be open to receive encouragement from others without feeling resentful or pressed.

Every truth you have appropriated for yourself about your new life in Christ is equally true for other Christians. Your responsibility is to point them to those truths:

They are not alone.
He is with them.
He is the strength of their life.
There is no condemnation for those in Christ Jesus.
God will meet their needs according to His riches in Christ
    Jesus.

You can point them to the truth of God's Word so they can believe and speak victoriously instead of confessing misery, failure, doubt and defeat. You can speak to them in the name of Jesus, saying what He wants to say to encourage them.

Jesus says, 'if two of you on earth agree about anything you ask for, it will be done for you by my Father in heaven' (Matt. 18:19). By this Jesus means that the two people should agree in their hearts about what they believe; they are in complete harmony about the matter. They do not merely agree to a formula of words, one praying a prayer, the other saying, 'Amen'! What they pray comes from their heart-conviction as to what God will do about the matter.

It is good to talk together with others and allow the Holy Spirit to bring you to a common mind as to what you are to believe. Whatever you agree together in *faith* will be done by your Father in heaven. When you arrive at a common mind, you can pray with confidence, knowing that 'it will be done for you'.

Honesty is vital here, both with God and with yourself, especially if faith is lacking at first. An honest admission of unbelief gives another person opportunity to speak faith to you and show you what the Lord promises in His Word. As you hear the truth together through one another your confidence is strengthened. You can encourage faith in others and they can encourage faith in you. When one wavers the other can remain strong. We need each other in our faith walk with the Lord.

Hear now the words of Jesus. Allow His truth to fill your heart. His prayer promises are for *you*.

---

**Meditation:**
IF TWO OF YOU ON EARTH AGREE ABOUT ANYTHING YOU ASK FOR, IT WILL BE DONE FOR YOU BY MY FATHER IN HEAVEN (MATT. 18:19).

Therefore encourage one another and build each other up (1 THESS. 5:11).

And whatever you do, whether in word or deed, do it all in the name of the Lord Jesus (COL. 3:17).

**Praise:**
May the peoples praise you, O God; may all the peoples praise you (PS. 67:3).

# PART FOUR

# YOUR LIFE OF FAITH

# 27. *Faith in God*

'Have faith in God' (MARK 11:22).

Holy Spirit, help me to have faith in God at all times.

> **READING:** MARK 11:22–5
> 'Have faith in God,' Jesus answered. 'I tell you the truth, if anyone says to this mountain, "Go, throw yourself into the sea," and does not doubt in his heart but believes that what he says will happen, it will be done for him. Therefore I tell you, whatever you ask for in prayer, believe that you have received it, and it will be yours. And when you stand praying, if you hold anything against anyone, forgive him, so that your Father in heaven may forgive you your sins.'

---

Jesus teaches His disciples to pray with faith. First, He says, it is important to have faith in God. That might seem self-evident, but it is only too easy to concentrate on the need or problem, on your feelings or fears. If you do this, faith rapidly drains away.

To have faith in God is to have faith in His Word. Your faith in Jesus demonstrates you are able to believe without seeing. Doubting Thomas refused to believe Jesus had risen until he saw Him for Himself. When he saw he worshipped, saying, '"My Lord and my God!" Then Jesus told him, "Because you have seen me, you have believed; blessed are those who have not seen and yet have believed"' (John 20:28–9).

So you are a blessed one. You believe without seeing. When you pray with faith, God wants you to believe in the result of your prayer before there is anything to see. The world says: See and then believe. Jesus says: Believe and then see!

As you receive the Word, see with the eyes of faith the answer to your need. You can end every prayer with thanksgiving because you believe the Father answers you, whether you are praying for yourself or for someone else. 'Do not be anxious about anything, but in everything, by prayer and petition, with thanksgiving, present your requests to God' (Phil. 4:6).

This is how Jesus Himself prayed. He stood before the tomb of Lazarus and said: 'Father, I thank you that you have heard me. I knew that you always hear me' (John 11:41–2). He said this *before* Lazarus was raised. This is the confidence that comes from knowing the faithfulness of your Father in heaven.

You have this relationship because you are a child of God. You can be so confident of your Father's desire to give to you that you can be still at any moment and in any place, and receive from Him through His Word and by His Spirit. You have faith in God. He hears you and meets with you every time you wait on Him.

Hear Jesus encouraging you now, urging you to exercise your faith in God, for He knows His Father will never fail you.

---

**Meditation:**
HAVE FAITH IN GOD (MARK 11:22).

According to your faith will it be done to you (MATT. 9:29).

Trust in God; trust also in me (JOHN 14:1).

**Praise:**
Then they believed his promises and sang his praise (PS. 106:12).

# 28. Speak to the Mountains

'Jesus replied, "I tell you truth, if you have faith and do not doubt, not only can you do what was done to the fig tree, but also you can say to this mountain, 'Go, throw yourself into the sea,' and it will be done"' (MATT. 21:21).

Lord, I want to learn to speak to mountains and see them moved.

---

**READING:** MARK 11:22–5
'Have faith in God,' Jesus answered. 'I tell you the truth, if anyone says to this mountain, "Go, throw yourself into the sea," and does not doubt in his heart but believes that what he says will happen, it will be done for him. Therefore I tell you, whatever you ask for in prayer, believe that you have received it, and it will be yours. And when you stand praying, if you hold anything against anyone, forgive him, so that your Father in heaven may forgive you your sins.'

---

Do you speak to your problems? Jesus tells you to do so. He says you are to speak to the mountains and command them to move. Obviously these are not physical mountains of rock, but mountains of need, the problems that have to be removed from your life.

Faith gives you confidence to speak to the mountains in your life. God has not put them there, and He wants them removed. Wrong thinking leads to unbelief. If you imagine your problems come from God, you will not have faith to ask Him to take them away, nor will you have confidence to speak to the needs.

It is the enemy who wants to put hindrances in your way. Jesus wants you to exercise your authority over all the power of the devil. If you resist him, he will flee from you. If you come against the mountains he puts in your way, you can command them to be thrown into the sea.

Sometimes Christians accept their problems instead of coming against them in faith. The devil loves such passive attitudes. Even as you pray, receiving the Spirit and life in God's Word know that you are coming against these mountains with all His resources behind you. The mountains must give way. God's power is greater than any need.

There is a kind of godly indignation at the spoiling tactics of the enemy. Instead of passively accepting problems, Christians should rise up in indignation against the negative things which cause upset, pain and chaos in people's lives. Jesus expressed such indignation against the Pharisees, against the money-lenders in the temple, against demonic forces and sickness, and against the devil himself.

You can speak to the mountains in your experience with all the authority of one who lives in Christ. You are given the privilege of speaking in His name, on His behalf, in the way He would speak to the problems you encounter. See them as He would see them, and deal with them as He would.

Listen to these words of Jesus. He is saying *you* can speak to the particular mountain before you and it will be moved. Don't believe in the mountain: trust Him.

---

**Meditation:**
YOU CAN SAY TO THIS MOUNTAIN, 'GO, THROW YOURSELF INTO THE SEA,' AND IT WILL BE DONE (MATT. 21:21).

Nothing will be impossible for you (MATT. 17:21).

Everything is possible for him who believes (MARK 9:23).

**Praise:**
Every day I will praise you and extol your name for ever and ever (PS. 145:2).

# 29. Believe you have Received

'If you believe, you will receive whatever you ask for in prayer' (MATT. 21:22).

Father, I want to pray always with faith.

**READING:** MARK 11:22–5
'Have faith in God,' Jesus answered. 'I tell you the truth, if anyone says to this mountain, "Go, throw yourself into the sea," and does not doubt in his heart but believes that what he says will happen, it will be done for him. Therefore I tell you, whatever you ask for in prayer, believe that you have received it, and it will be yours. And when you stand praying, if you hold anything against anyone, forgive him, so that your Father in heaven may forgive you your sins.'

---

The enemy will try to persuade you that you do not have enough faith to be able to receive from God. Don't listen to him! You do have faith. You believe God wants to give to you and every time you pray in this way you are able to receive from Him.

To pray with faith is not to say that God will do something at some time in the future. That is hope, not faith. When you pray with faith, you believe you have received it.

This type of prayer helps you greatly in this respect. You believe God is giving to you as you receive His Word in prayer. Although the total answer to your need may not be manifested immediately, nevertheless you believe the outcome is already settled. You have received your answer by faith and every time you pray like this you are appropriating your answer.

It is great when God meets with us in miraculous ways, when needs, even of a critical or substantial nature, are met spontaneously. But this is not the only way God answers prayer, neither is it the only way of receiving from Him.

I receive some answers immediately, but others come gradually. This is true of healing, for example. I see God heal many people spontaneously, but I hear of many others who receive their healing over a period of time. This is true of medically incurable diseases, or of more minor matters.

Faith does not question the final outcome. You believe you have received the total answer, even though this may be manifested gradually. Every occasion of receiving through prayer is a further step towards the ultimate victory.

Come against the need in your life. Speak to the mountain and command that it be moved. The Lord does not want you living with that problem; He wants it thrown into the sea and sunk without trace. With the eyes of faith, see this as accomplished, and know that every time you pray you receive the answer to your need.

Your Father hears you when you pray. He wants you to be so sure of His love and faithfulness, to have such faith in the power of His Word, that every time you pray you believe you receive from Him.

---

**Meditation:**
IF YOU BELIEVE, YOU WILL RECEIVE WHATEVER YOU ASK FOR IN PRAYER (MATT. 21:22).

And I will do whatever you ask in my name, so that the Son may bring glory to the Father (JOHN 14:13).

You may ask me for anything in my name, and I will do it (JOHN 14:14).

**Praise:**
Trust in the Lord for ever, for the Lord, the Lord, is the Rock eternal (ISA. 26:4).

# 30. Receiving

'And when you stand praying, if you hold anything against anyone, forgive him, so that your Father in heaven may forgive you your sins' (MARK 11:25).

Holy Spirit, help me always to have a forgiving attitude.

**READING:** MATTHEW 18:21–35
Then Peter came to Jesus and asked, 'Lord, how many times shall I forgive my brother when he sins against me? Up to seven times?' Jesus answered, 'I tell you, not seven times, but seventy-seven times.

'Therefore, the kingdom of heaven is like a king who wanted to settle accounts with his servants. As he began the settlement, a man who owed him ten thousand talents was brought to him. Since he was not able to pay, the master ordered that he and his wife and his children and all that he had be sold to repay the debt.

'The servant fell on his knees before him. "Be patient with me," he begged, "and I will pay back everything." The servant's master took pity on him, cancelled the debt and let him go.

'But when that servant went out, he found one of his fellow servants who owed him a hundred denarii. He grabbed him and began to choke him. "Pay back what you owe me!" he demanded.

'His fellow servant fell to his knees and begged him, "Be patient with me, and I will pay you back."

'But he refused. Instead, he went off and had the man thrown into prison until he could pay the debt. When the other servants saw what had happened, they were greatly distressed and went and told their master everything that had happened.

'Then the master called the servant in. "You wicked

servant," he said, "I cancelled all that debt of yours because you begged me to. Shouldn't you have had mercy on your fellow servant just as I had on you?" In anger his master turned him over to the jailers until he should pay back all he owed.

'This is how my heavenly Father will treat each of you unless you forgive your brother from your heart.'

Jesus made it very clear how important it is to forgive: 'For if you forgive men when they sin against you, your heavenly Father will also forgive you. But if you do not forgive men their sins, your Father will not forgive your sins' (Matt. 6:14–15).

If you do not forgive, you are not yourself forgiven, and if you are not forgiven it is extremely difficult to receive from God, no matter how much faith you have. Forgiveness is an expression of love and mercy from God to you. And He expects you to extend similar love and mercy towards others. Paul warns, 'if I have a faith that can move mountains, but have not love, I am nothing' (1 Cor. 13:2).

Jesus told the parable of the unmerciful servant to warn us of the consequences of refusing to forgive others.

In your preparation to receive, ask God to forgive you *and extend your forgiveness towards others*. You are to maintain an attitude of mercy no matter how many times you have to forgive. Forgiveness needs to become a natural reaction when others wrong you. Instead of burning with anger or resentment, forgive. Instead of waiting until the other apologises before forgiving, have a forgiving attitude immediately you are aware of the wrong, so that the sore has no opportunity to fester.

*Whenever* you pray you are to forgive, that is what Jesus says. Not sometimes, but *whenever*: and whenever means every time you pray.

I have known many to receive healing of physical or emotional needs as a result of forgiving others. No doubt the Lord wanted to release their healing to them before, but the lack of forgiveness prevented this. For example, a woman in the advanced stages of multiple sclerosis came to a meeting in her wheel-chair. Through the preaching the Lord convicted her of her need to forgive someone who had caused a deep hurt in her life. From that moment she began to be healed of her disease. She was soon out of her wheel-chair and walking around normally.

No one prayed with her; Jesus ministered His Word to her heart. When she responded she was set free. 'Forgive us our debts, as we also have forgiven our debtors' (Matt. 6:12).

Let the words of this meditation become part of you, so that on every occasion your instinctive reaction is to forgive. You are to forgive – as the Lord forgave you. He never wants to withhold that forgiveness from you if you do not withhold your forgiveness from others.

---

**Meditation:**
FORGIVE AS THE LORD FORGAVE YOU (COL. 3:13).

If you hold anything against anyone, forgive him (MARK 11:25).

For if you forgive men when they sin against you, your heavenly Father will also forgive you (MATT. 6:14).

**Praise:**
As far as the east is from the west, so far has he removed our transgressions from us (PS. 103:12).

# 31. Acting out your Faith

'Then Jesus said, "Did I not tell you that if you believed, you would see the glory of God?"' (JOHN 11:40).

Father, may I know your faithfulness in always answering my prayer.

**READING:** JOHN 11:40–2
Then Jesus said, 'Did I not tell you that if you believed, you would see the glory of God?'
So they took away the stone. Then Jesus looked up and said, 'Father, I thank you that you have heard me. I knew that you always hear me, but I said this for the benefit of the people standing here, that they may believe that you sent me.'

---

Faith is not a feeling; it is an activity. Faith is expressed in what you say and do. Jesus says that from the overflow of the heart the mouth speaks. If there is faith in your heart, your mouth will proclaim that faith, and your actions will declare it.

When Jesus heard that His great friend Lazarus was sick, His immediate reaction was one of faith: 'This sickness will not end in death' (John 11:4). This is His faith reaction to the news. The enemy might want to steal the life of His beloved friend through sickness, but he will not be allowed to prevail. This is a statement of faith, and of godly indignation!

Because there is faith in His heart, Jesus does not hurry to the scene. With His eyes of faith He sees Lazarus being raised long before the event. It is four days before He arrives at the tomb. Each of His actions demonstrates the reality of His faith. '"Take away the stone," he said' (John 11:38). What would be the point of saying this unless He expected a miracle?

He is concerned to see God glorified: 'This sickness will not end in death. No, it is for God's glory so that God's Son may be glorified through it' (John 11:4). 'Did I not tell you that if you believed, you would see the glory of God?' (John 11:40).

He wants to see His Father glorified in the situation – Satan's seeming triumph will be turned to defeat. His Father's glory will be reflected in the Son as He proceeds with faith.

He stands before the tomb and prays: 'Father, I thank you that you have heard me. I knew that you always hear me, but I said this for the benefit of the people standing here, that they may believe that you sent me' (John 11:41–2).

This is prayer with faith. Jesus knows His Father always hears Him. He believes He has received His answer before there is anything to show for such confidence. The way in which He prays is an example to all those around.

Then He speaks to the 'mountain' with a word of authority: 'Lazarus, come out!' (John 11:43). And he does!

Remember what Jesus teaches, 'believe that you have received it, and it will be yours' (Mark 11:24). Do you see how this principle operates in practice? Jesus has faith; He is confident of the outcome from the very beginning. He knows in His heart what will happen.

You may not have to raise the dead very often, but every day you need to pray with faith. Remember, it is not only what you say at the time of prayer that matters. Like Jesus, you need to have faith attitudes in your heart. All your words and actions are to spring from these heart attitudes. Faith that is an external veneer is not real faith! It is the prayer and desire of the heart that God promises to answer.

You are about to pray to the Father with the words of Jesus. Because you live in Him, these words are as true for you as for Him. Your heavenly Father always hears you, and He promises to answer the cry of your heart.

---

**Meditation:**
FATHER, I THANK YOU THAT YOU HAVE HEARD ME. I KNOW THAT YOU ALWAYS HEAR ME (JOHN 11:41–2).

How much more will your Father in heaven give good gifts to those who ask him! (MATT. 7:11).

To your name be the glory, because of your love and faithfulness (PS. 115:1).

**Praise:**
This is the assurance we have in approaching God: that if we ask anything according to his will, he hears us. And if we know that he hears us – whatever we ask – we know that we have what we asked of Him (1 JOHN 5:14–15).

# 32. *Faithful Speech*

'Make a tree good and its fruit will be good, or make a tree bad and its fruit will be bad, for a tree is recognised by its fruit' (MATT. 12:33).

Holy Spirit, help me to speak positive words of faith.

**READING:** MATTHEW 12:35–7
The good man brings good things out of the good stored up in him, and the evil man brings evil things out of the evil stored up in him. But I tell you that men will have to give account on the day of judgment for every careless word they have spoken. For by your words you will be acquitted, and by your words you will be condemned.

These are some of the most awesome words Jesus spoke, and they point to the importance of the way in which we use our mouths. James warns us: 'With the tongue we praise our Lord and Father, and with it we curse men, who have been made in God's likeness. Out of the same mouth come praise and cursing. My brothers, this should not be. Can both fresh water and salt water flow from the same spring?' (Jas. 3:9–11).

The way you speak indicates what you believe. If you are full of positive faith, your mouth will speak positive words. If you are full of fear and unbelief you will speak negatively. If you are double-minded you will speak in confusion, vacillating from faith to doubt and back to faith again, not sure what you really believe.

A good tree can only produce good fruit. A positive heart can only produce positive words of faith and encouragement. A praising heart will rejoice in the Lord, regardless of the circumstances. What is happening around the person will not change his heart attitudes.

There is an important lesson to learn here, for many speak as if their problems cause their negative responses. This is not the case; the problem has simply revealed the negative heart attitude already there. It has not created the negative reaction, only revealed it. What has been hidden in the dark has been drawn out into the light.

For this reason two people can react in entirely different ways to identical circumstances. One will immediately be dejected and frustrated, fearful and angry even. Another will look to Jesus, entrusting the matter into His hands, confident He will not fail. It all depends on what is already in the heart.

This is why it is so important to store the truth of God's Word in your heart, so that it may be a wellspring of life within you. If the truth is already in your heart, your mouth will proclaim it. Your words will be like the sounding of a true note in harmony with God's Word, rather than one which is out of tune, at discord with His will.

The answer to fear and doubt is not to ask the Lord to remove them; rather begin to make a positive confession. There is no condemnation in being attacked by negative doubts; this is Satan's work and he loves to try and undermine the faith of God's children. The way to overcome him is to resist him in the way Jesus did: 'It is written . . .' (Luke 4:4, 8, 10).

You will find that to speak the positive truth of God's Word will help that Word live in you. As you declare it, believe it. This is what God says about the matter. You will experience positive results as you steadfastly maintain that confession in the face of all the difficulties. This is much more powerful than expressing the negatives of the world, the flesh and the devil.

Store the good things within you – and good things will flow out of you. God has given you a mouth. You have the ability to speak the negative words of unbelief, fear and sickness; or, like Jesus, you can speak the positive words of faith.

---

**Meditation:**
LET THE WORD OF CHRIST DWELL IN YOU RICHLY (COL. 3:16).

Above all else, guard your heart, for it is the wellspring of life (PROV. 4:23).

Keep my commands in your heart, for they will prolong your life many years and bring you prosperity (PROV. 3:1–2).

**Praise:**
I will sing of the Lord's great love for ever; with my mouth I will make your faithfulness known through all generations (PS. 89:1).

# 33. Hold Fast

'[My words] are life to those who find them and health to a man's whole body' (PROV. 4:22).

Father, I believe you will watch over your Word to perform it in my life.

**READING:** LUKE 8:11–15
This is the meaning of the parable: The seed is the word of God. Those along the path are the ones who hear, and then the devil comes and takes away the word from their hearts, so that they cannot believe and be saved. Those on the rock are the ones who receive the word with joy when they hear it, but they have no root. They believe for a while, but in the time of testing they fall away. The seed that fell among thorns stands for those who hear, but as they go on their way they are choked by life's worries, riches and pleasures, and they do not mature. But the seed on good soil stands for those with a noble and good heart, who hear the word, retain it, and by persevering produce a crop.

---

God will never deny His Word, but will perform what He has promised. Often your experience does not measure up to these promises, but God wants to raise your experience to the level of His Word, not reduce His Word to the level of your experience. There is no room for question-marks as to God's will when He clearly expresses His purpose in His Word. God's will never contradict His Word. If God was ever to deny His Word, He would deny His Son. That He will never do for He is not divided against Himself. He will honour the covenant, the binding agreement, He has made with His children and which is sealed, or ratified, with the precious blood of Jesus.

God wants you to take Him at His Word. If you believe what He says, you will hold fast to His Words with all your heart, even in the face of adverse circumstances.

Abraham inherited God's promises by faith with patience. Jesus never promised instantaneous answers to all our prayers. Often patient endurance is needed until the promise is fulfilled, and that can be the real test of faith. During the waiting period you need to continue to receive His Words, and hold fast *with an honest and good heart*.

Every time you waver in your faith, you have to come back to God and confess your doubt. He will forgive you and you can return to the positive affirmation of His truth, praising Him for His faithfulness.

Nobody can prevent God from doing what He says He is going to do. This is why it is so important to hear Him speaking His words of promise to your heart. He watches over His Word to perform it. Those who bear a hundredfold fruit in Jesus's parable are those 'who hear the word, retain it, and by persevering produce a crop' (Luke 8:15).

---

**Meditation:**
I THE LORD HAVE SPOKEN, AND I WILL DO IT (EZEK. 36:36).

The Lord is faithful to all his promises (PS. 145:13).

God, who has called you into fellowship with his Son Jesus Christ our Lord, is faithful (1 COR. 1:9).

**Praise:**
My son, do not forget my teaching, but keep my commands in your heart, for they will prolong your life many years and bring you prosperity (PROV. 3:1–2).

# 34. The Lord your Healer

'I am the Lord who heals you' (EXOD. 15:26).

Father, I want to know you as my healer.

**READING:** LUKE 4:14–21
Jesus returned to Galilee in the power of the Spirit, and news about him spread through the whole countryside. He taught in their synagogues, and everyone praised him.

He went to Nazareth, where he had been brought up, and on the Sabbath day he went into the synagogue, as was his custom. And he stood up to read. The scroll of the prophet Isaiah was handed to him. Unrolling it, he found the place where it is written:

'The Spirit of the Lord is on me, because he has anointed me to preach good news to the poor. He has sent me to proclaim freedom for the prisoners and recovery of sight for the blind, to release the oppressed, to proclaim the year of the Lord's favour.'

Then he rolled up the scroll, gave it back to the attendant and sat down. The eyes of everyone in the synagogue were fastened on him, and he began by saying to them, 'Today this scripture is fulfilled in your hearing.'

---

It is God's nature to heal. He revealed himself to Israel as the Lord who heals. Jesus came to do the will of His Father; He did only the things He saw His Father doing – and He spent much of His public ministry healing the sick. When He went to the cross He made provision for our total healing, spirit, soul and body.

Jesus expressed the Father's desire to heal. In one sense all God does in our lives is part of His healing purpose, saving us from sin, sickness, poverty and death. His Words are words of healing, 'they are life to those who find them and health to a man's whole body' (Prov. 4:22).

You can receive healing every time you sit down quietly and 'receive' His Words into your spirit. Hear the Lord speak to your heart saying, 'I am the Lord who heals you.' Know that these are not words *about* healing; they are words *of* healing. Yes, God's healing power can come to you through His Word.

Understand that the Lord is speaking to you personally: 'I am the Lord who heals *you*.' And He is conveying His healing life and power to you as you receive His Words.

In times of particular need, you can spend a few minutes several times a day receiving healing from the Lord as you receive His Words of healing in this way. Remember, faith comes from hearing the Word of Christ proclaimed to your heart. It may seem little is happening at first. But there will come the point at which the Spirit will declare those words of truth to your heart. At that moment they become personal to you; they are the voice of God to you.

As you pray, believe that the Holy Spirit comes upon you to bring God's healing into your life and body. Both the Word and the Spirit are agencies of God's healing grace to you. What a combination when you bring the two together!

What is more, the Holy Spirit will work through you to bring healing to others, to members of your family, to friends and fellow Christians. Teach them to be still, to hear the Lord speak words of healing to their hearts. You may feel it right to help them by laying hands on them, praying for the Holy Spirit to come upon them to heal. Whether you do this or not, know there is healing life and power in God's Words and He is going to speak healing into your life now.

---

**Meditation:**
I AM THE LORD WHO HEALS YOU (EXOD. 15:26).

He drove out the spirits with a word and healed all the sick (MATT. 8:16).

But just say the word, and my servant will be healed
(MATT. 8:8).

**Praise:**
I trust in the Lord. I will be glad and rejoice in your
love, for you saw my affliction and knew the anguish
of my soul (PS. 31:6–7).

# 35. Health

'By his wounds you have been healed' (1 PET. 2:24).

Jesus, I need the revelation in my heart that I am healed by
your wounds.

### READING: ISAIAH 53:4–10
Surely he took up our infirmities and carried our
sorrows, yet we considered him stricken by God,
smitten by him, and afflicted. But he was pierced for
our transgressions, he was crushed for our iniquities;
the punishment that brought us peace was upon him,
and by his wounds we are healed. We all, like sheep,
have gone astray, each of us has turned to his own way;
and the Lord has laid on him the iniquity of us all.

He was oppressed and afflicted, yet he did not open
his mouth; he was led like a lamb to the slaughter, and
as a sheep before her shearers is silent, so he did not
open his mouth. By oppression and judgment, he was
taken away. And who can speak of his descendants?
For he was cut off from the land of the living; for the
transgression of my people he was stricken. He was
assigned a grave with the wicked, and with the rich in
his death, though he had done no violence, nor was
any deceit in his mouth.

Yet it was the Lord's will to crush him and cause him

to suffer, and though the Lord makes his life a guilt offering, he will see his offspring and prolong his days, and the will of the Lord will prosper in his hand.

---

When a need for healing arises in your life it is easy to speak negatively about the dreadful pain, the discomfort and the weakness. The more you concentrate on the problem, the more you place yourself in the grip of that problem. You believe in your heart what your mouth speaks. How much healthier to speak words of healing because the truth is stored in your heart.

There are several ways of receiving healing through Jesus. The key is to understand that He dealt with your need on the cross. 'Surely he took up our infirmities and carried our sorrows.' He dealt with every emotional and physical need as well as all our spiritual needs.

Jesus took up your infirmities and sorrows. He was rejected and oppressed so that you may be set free from rejection and oppression. He suffered for you in order to free you. By His wounds you are healed in every way, in spirit, soul and body. Affirm for yourself:

### By His stripes I am healed.

You do not need to see yourself as 'Poor me'. Neither are you to feel condemned for being sick. Here is an opportunity to see the manifestation of the victory of the healing of Jesus, won for you on the cross. You need to make the positive confession of faith in God's power and will to heal you. Without that confession which stems from faith, you may well deprive yourself of your healing, no matter how often you ask others to pray for you. God hears the prayer of your heart and He knows what you really believe. Faith does not say, 'God will heal me.' Faith says: 'By His wounds I have been healed'; He has done it.

This truth needs to be revelation in your heart. Know that every time you sit down and receive the words of healing,

God's healing is actually taking place in you. Affirm the truth: *Jesus has carried my infirmities and my sorrows.*

You do not need to question whether it is God's desire to heal you. Instead you can affirm: 'In Christ, He has met my need.' Through His mercy and by the power of the Holy Spirit you are able to receive His healing. As you repeat this Scripture know that the Lord is conveying healing to you personally.

Remember, He often heals from the inside outwards. You may experience considerable healing within you before you see all the physical needs met. Whatever way He works in your situation, you can be thankful that by the wounds of Jesus you have been healed.

Do not be discouraged if your healing does not take place instantaneously or in a miraculous fashion. Some healings take place like that, others take a period of time. Nobody manifests the perfect healing of spirit, soul and body during this life; but as you feed on God's Word His healing purposes are being furthered in your experience.

---

**Meditation:**
BY HIS WOUNDS YOU HAVE BEEN HEALED (1 PET. 2:24).

Surely he took up our infirmities and carried our sorrows (ISA. 53:4).

Go! It will be done just as you believed it would (MATT. 8:13).

**Praise:**
One generation will commend your works to another; they will tell of your mighty acts (PS. 145:4).

---

NB. For a further treatment of the whole subject of healing see the author's book, *Receive Your Healing*.

# 36. The Holy Spirit Helps

'When the Counsellor comes, whom I will send to you from the Father, the Spirit of truth who goes out from the Father, he will testify about me' (JOHN 15:26).

Holy Spirit, please fill me with your healing life and power.

**READING:** JOHN 16:12–15
I have much more to say to you, more than you can now bear. But when he, the Spirit of truth, comes, he will guide you into all truth. He will not speak on his own; he will speak only what he hears, and he will tell you what is yet to come. He will bring glory to me by taking from what is mine and making it known to you. All that belongs to the Father is mine. That is why I said the Spirit will take from what is mine and make it known to you.

The Holy Spirit will help you to confess the positive truth of God's Word. This is part of His job, of His ministry to you. 'But the Counsellor, the Holy Spirit, whom the Father will send in my name, will teach you all things and will remind you of everything I have said to you' (John 14:26).

Do not feel condemned when attacked by the negative. The Holy Spirit will bring to your mind the positive truths that will counteract the negative.

If you feel afraid, speak out the positive words of faith, such as, 'I am with you always'. When you live faith and learn to confess the Word in faith, you will find yourself beginning to live in a new dimension, no longer believing experiences and waiting passively for the next problem. You appreciate that you live in Christ and He in you, and you have available from God all the resources needed to meet every situation.

If you speak need, you have need. If you speak as one provided for, you will see the Lord's provision.

If you speak sickness, you will remain sick. If you speak healing, you will experience healing.

If you speak despair, you will feel everything is hopeless. If you speak encouragement, you will be encouraged yourself and will appreciate that God is able to meet with you in every situation.

These are not formulae of speech to be repeated mechanically, for the words you speak need to flow from the heart. This is why it is so important to receive the positive truth of God's Word into your heart.

Pray for the Holy Spirit to help you in this. You are not expected to struggle on in your own strength, but to flow in His power. He will help you. It is His job, His desire to do so. Call on the Holy Spirit any moment of the day or night – and He will help you. He will declare God's Word to you, bringing to the conscious level of your mind the truth you need to be reminded of at that particular time.

Hear Jesus speak to you now the words He spoke to His disciples. Let Him breathe His Spirit into you afresh. Believe He is doing that as you pray.

---

**Meditation:**
RECEIVE THE HOLY SPIRIT (JOHN 20:22).

The Holy Spirit . . . will remind you of everything I have said to you (JOHN 14:26).

The Spirit will take from what is mine and make it known to you (JOHN 16:15).

**Praise:**
The Lord has done great things for us, and we are filled with joy (PS. 126:3).

# 37. Authority over Satan

'The one who is in you is greater than the one who is in the world' (1 JOHN 4:4).

Lord Jesus, I want to exercise the authority you give me over the evil one.

**READING:** 1 JOHN 4:2–5
This is how you can recognise the Spirit of God: Every spirit that acknowledges that Jesus Christ has come in the flesh is from God, but every spirit that does not acknowledge Jesus is not from God. This is the spirit of the antichrist, which you have heard is coming and even now is already in the world.

You, dear children, are from God and have overcome them, because the one who is in you is greater than the one who is in the world. They are from the world and therefore speak from the viewpoint of the world, and the world listens to them.

---

When Jesus was led by the Spirit of God into the wilderness and Satan came to tempt Him, Jesus dismissed him with the Word of God. Learn to do this. You have the authority to dismiss him as your defeated enemy. With the spiritual armour God gives you, He fills both your hands. In one hand you hold the shield of faith 'with which you can extinguish all the flaming arrows of the evil one' (Eph. 6:16). With that shield in position you say to the enemy, 'I'm not going to listen to any of your accusations or lies.' In the other hand you have the sword of the Spirit which is the Word of God. These are the words of truth which are powerful and to which Satan has no answer. He knows the truth of those words.

But Satan is glorified when your speech disagrees with God's Word. Because he is the father of all lies, he delights to hear Christians making negative statements. In his role as deceiver and accuser he tries to persuade you to doubt the promises of God and concentrate on your unworthiness before God. He wants to deceive you into contradicting the truths of Scripture.

The Spirit is the one who is always declaring God to you in the here and now. He is wanting you to look up and to look forward, not to look back or look in on yourself. Satan, however, feeds all the negative things that are there within you. He could score a victory now if you allow him to make you feel condemned by all the negative confessions you have made. But you know the truth: 'Therefore, there is now no condemnation for those who are in Christ Jesus' (Rom. 8:1).

God has forgiven all your past failures and wants you now to live in the power of His Word. No longer are you going to live as the victim of your feelings and fears. You are not merely on the defensive expecting one attack after another; you are moving on to the offensive against the enemy. 'The weapons we fight with are not the weapons of the world. On the contrary, they have divine power to demolish strongholds. We demolish arguments and every pretension that sets itself up against the knowledge of God, and we take captive every thought to make it obedient to Christ' (2 Cor. 10:4–5).

You believe the Spirit of God, not the lies of the enemy. As you pray the Spirit will witness to your heart the truths you repeat to yourself again and again. It is by the Holy Spirit's activity that these become part of you and He will bring them to your consciousness whenever you have need, the right Word for the right occasion.

The Spirit of God within you is greater than the power of the enemy. As a believer you have been given authority over all the works of the devil. Don't let him kick you around. Show him who is boss! Exercise the authority you have been given.

---

**Meditation:**
I HAVE GIVEN YOU AUTHORITY . . . TO OVERCOME ALL THE POWER OF THE ENEMY; NOTHING WILL HARM YOU (LUKE 10:19).

Resist the devil, and he will flee from you (JAS. 4:7).

He . . . gave them authority to drive out evil spirits and to heal every disease and sickness (MATT. 10:1).

**Praise:**
From the lips of children and infants you have ordained praise because of your enemies, to silence the foe and the avenger (PS. 8:2).

# 38. *Watered with Praise*

'Serve the Lord with gladness; come before him with joyful songs. Know that the Lord is God. It is he who made us, and we are his; we are his people, the sheep of his pasture' (PS. 100:2–3).

Holy Spirit, may there be a continual song of praise in my heart.

**READING:** PSALM 34:1–3
I will extol the Lord at all times; his praise will always be on my lips. My soul will boast in the Lord; let the afflicted hear and rejoice. Glorify the Lord with me: let us exalt his name together.

---

Your prayer to God is like a seed of faith that you plant and which needs to be watered with praise. Praise concentrates on the Lord Himself, rather than His gifts and blessings to us. The more your attention is fixed on Him, the more you are able to understand that He is far bigger than your situation or need. You can rejoice in Him and in His victory and provision made possible through Jesus. The more you know the Lord, the more you will want to praise Him; and the more you praise

Him, the more you will know Him. Those who express a dislike for praise betray their lack of relationship with Jesus.

Praise is a way of life. It is far more than singing hymns and spiritual songs to the Lord; it is an activity of the whole being and is to be expressed in every area of your life.

David was a man who could experience the depths of despair and desolation; yet when surrounded by his enemies, with the situation looking disastrous, he could say: 'Why are you downcast, O my soul? Why so disturbed within me? Put your hope in God, for I will yet praise him, my Saviour and my God' (Ps. 42:11).

God's love for you is steadfast, certain and sure: He is always worthy of your praise. The essence of worship is to express to God what He is worth. Whether you feel like praising or worshipping Him or not, He is worthy of your praise. There will be times when you are conscious of God's light and times when all *appears* dark and difficult. God, though, is light all the time; in Him there is never any darkness. Even when He is revealing some area of darkness in you in order to deal with it, His light remains undiminished. Praise directs your attention away from yourself, your negative feelings and any darkness you may experience.

The darker the situation, the more in need you are of God's light; the greater therefore you need to praise Him. And yet this is the very opposite to what many people do. The greater the difficulty, the less they feel inclined to praise. Instead they concentrate on the problem and their own feelings.

Praise needs to be continuous in your Christian life because it is so easy to look in on yourself, and analyse yourself instead of allowing the Spirit to direct your focus to the light and glory of God in the wonder of praise.

Do not listen to the lies of the enemy. He suggests that it would not be real to praise God unless you felt like it. He will even suggest it will be hypocritical to do so. How the deceiver can deceive! He will do anything to try and prevent you from praising the Lord and focusing your attention on Him.

It is good to read one or two psalms of praise whenever you begin to pray, particularly when you feel prayer is difficult. This method of meditation centres your heart and mind on the

Lord Himself, and that helps to put your own situation in proper perspective. No matter what your circumstances He loves you, cares for you and wants the best for you.

**Meditation:**
PRAISE THE LORD, O MY SOUL; ALL MY INMOST BEING, PRAISE HIS HOLY NAME (PS. 103:1).

Rejoice in the Lord always. I will say it again: Rejoice! (PHIL. 4:4).

Be joyful always; pray continually; give thanks in all circumstances, for this is God's will for you in Christ Jesus (1 THESS. 5:16–18).

**Praise:**
Let everything that has breath praise the Lord (PS. 150:6).

# 39. *Victory*

'But thanks be to God! He gives us the victory through our Lord Jesus Christ' (1 COR. 15:57).

Lord Jesus, I want to live as one who is more than a conqueror because of your victory.

**READING:** ROMANS 8:31–9
What, then, shall we say in response to this? If God is for us, who can be against us? He who did not spare His own Son, but gave him up for us all – how will he not also, along with him, graciously give us all things?

117

Who will bring any charge against those whom God has chosen? It is God who justifies. Who is he that condemns? Christ Jesus, who died – more than that, who was raised to life – is at the right hand of God and is also interceding for us. Who shall separate us from the love of Christ? Shall trouble or hardship or persecution or famine or nakedness or danger or sword? As it is written: 'For your sake we face death all day long; we are considered as sheep to be slaughtered.' No, in all these things we are more than conquerors through him who loved us. For I am convinced that neither death nor life, neither angels nor demons, neither the present nor the future, nor any powers, neither height nor depth, nor anything else in all creation, will be able to separate us from the love of God that is in Christ Jesus our Lord.

---

Confess the truth of God's Word to yourself: *I am more than a conqueror through Him who loves me!* What makes you more than a conqueror? You live in the victory Jesus has already achieved.

Nothing can separate you from the love of Christ. You can conquer 'trouble or hardship or persecution or famine or danger or sword' through Him. You have the victory over death and anything that comes against you in this life. Nothing in the present or the future can separate you from His love.

Jesus does not promise His followers an easy life. 'In this world you will have trouble,' He says; but continues by pointing them to the victory: 'But take heart! I have overcome the world' (John 16:33). When your faith is in Him, you overcome the world too. 'This is the victory that has overcome the world, even our faith. Who is it that overcomes the world? Only he who believes that Jesus is the Son of God' (1 John 5:4–5). You can exercise your faith and say confidently: *Through my faith in Jesus as God's Son I have overcome the world.*

No wonder Paul says God 'always leads us in triumphal procession in Christ' (2 Cor. 2:14). You cannot imagine Jesus leading us into failure or despair, pain or sickness, temptation or disaster. He leads God's children in the ways of peace and prosperity, of health and wholeness, of power and provision. Jesus did not come to support you in your need, but to supply your need. So you can affirm positively: *God always leads me in triumph.* If you know the truth, you can be confident, no matter how adverse the circumstances are. You can say to the God who never lies, 'Lord you are going to lead me in triumph. I am going to see your victory in this situation. Alleluia!' He promises, 'I will never leave you nor forsake you.' (Jos 1:5). So you can go forward with confidence; nothing can separate you from His love.

Look at the trials in your life as opportunities to see the victory of Jesus manifested again. God allows the trials to refine us, but he never wants us to be overcome by any situation. He has put the victory within our grasp.

The world sees the Church not as a body full of faith and power, but as a weak institution consisting of people with as many fears and anxieties as others. If we are born again into a new life in the Spirit, this is not the picture the world should have. People should see evidence of victory in our lives, as distinct from the despair and defeat of those outside Christ Jesus. Even in death a Christian is victorious because he is at one with the risen Christ. We only experience and manifest failure when we are not asserting our life in Christ and His life in us.

Hear the Word of God spoken to you personally by His Spirit. You are more than a conqueror through Jesus because of His love for you. You have a victorious faith that overcomes the world, the flesh and the devil!

---

**Meditation:**
NO, IN ALL THESE THINGS WE ARE MORE THAN CONQUERORS THROUGH HIM WHO LOVED US (ROM. 8:37).

But take heart! I have overcome the world (JOHN 16:33).

This is the victory that has overcome the world, even our faith (1 JOHN 5:4).

## Praise:
You give me your shield of victory, and your right hand sustains me (PS. 18:35).

# PART FIVE

# YOUR LIFE IN THE SPIRIT

# 40. A New Heart

'I will give you a new heart and put a new spirit in you; I will remove from you your heart of stone and give you a heart of flesh' (EZEK. 36:26).

Thank you, Father, for giving me a new heart.

**READING:** ROMANS 8:2–4
Through Christ Jesus the law of the Spirit of life set me free from the law of sin and death. For what the law was powerless to do in that it was weakened by the sinful nature, God did by sending his own Son in the likeness of sinful man to be a sin offering. And so he condemned sin in sinful man, in order that the righteous requirements of the law might be fully met in us, who do not live according to the sinful nature but according to the Spirit.

---

Under the Old Covenant, God revealed His purposes to His people through the commandments He gave them. But the law gave them no motivation or power to enable them to obey the Lord. Instead they chose to please themselves; to please God required such great effort and determination of will. Their hearts often became hardened against Him, because they wanted to satisfy their own desires instead.

Under the New Covenant, God promised to replace their stony hearts with new hearts. His law would no longer be written on tablets of stone, but on their new hearts. Then they will want to please Him.

The Lord has given you a brand new heart! You do not need to strive to please God in your own way; by the power of His Spirit you have His love and ability working within you. You have the heart to please Him and the ability to do so. You now have a heart that *desires* to praise, love and obey Him. 'I desire to do your will, O my God' (Ps. 40:8).

Paul says, 'the old has gone, the new has come!' (2 Cor. 5:17). God has taken away your old heart and given you a new one. Your old life without Jesus has ended; your new life in Him has begun. The deepest desire of the Spirit within you is to please the Lord – not out of a begrudging obedience, but out of a genuine longing to please Him. The Spirit of Jesus lives in your new heart, inspires your love for God and enables you to do what He desires. This spiritual heart wants to influence your soul (your mind, your will and your feelings), which have not yet become fully submitted to God. On occasions you still choose to please self instead of the Lord. This is walking in the flesh rather than the Spirit. What God puts into the heart has to radiate through the whole of your life.

The problem lies in the fact that you experience a mixture within yourself which leads to conflict. On the one hand you want to please self because of the self-love that persists in your life. On the other hand Jesus wants to bring you to the end of that self-love, for the more fully you submit yourself to Him, the more contented and peaceful you will become. Do not be surprised or alarmed at the conflict you experience within yourself. This is evidence that the Holy Spirit is doing His work within you, pointing you to the Word and the way of Jesus. Whenever you obey His prompting you bless Him; when you yield to the flesh, your natural instincts, you grieve Him. Even then you can turn back to Him seeking His forgiveness and submitting yourself afresh to His will.

Let the Lord renew His gift to you now. Hear His words of promise and know He is pouring the life of the Spirit into you as you pray.

---

**Meditation:**
I WILL GIVE YOU A NEW HEART AND PUT A NEW SPIRIT IN YOU (EZEK. 36:26).

Love the Lord your God with all your heart (MARK 12:30).

I am gentle and humble in heart (MATT. 11:29).

**Praise:**
Rejoice in the Lord, you who are righteous, and praise his holy name (PS. 97:12).

# 41. *The Role of the Holy Spirit*

'But when he, the Spirit of truth, comes, he will guide you into all truth' (JOHN 16:13).

Thank you, Holy Spirit, for living in me.

### READING: PSALM 51:10–13
Create in me a pure heart, O God, and renew a steadfast spirit within me. Do not cast me from your presence or take your Holy Spirit from me. Restore to me the joy of your salvation and grant me a willing spirit, to sustain me. Then I will teach transgressors your ways, and sinners will turn back to you.

---

Jesus tells us, 'the Spirit will take from what is mine and make it known to you' (John 16:15). Jesus also said the Holy Spirit 'will guide you into all truth' (John 16:13).

The Spirit will teach you everything – therefore you are to set your mind on the things of the Spirit. Paul tells the Romans: 'You, however, are controlled not by the sinful nature but by the Spirit, if the Spirit of God lives in you' (Rom. 8:9).

You do not have to allow your mind to be dominated by fleshly desires when you have the Spirit of God in your heart, wanting to guide your thoughts and speech to be consistent with His thoughts and words. In the old life you lived to please yourself; now you live to please Him. But if, even now, you set your mind on the sinful desires of the flesh you will grieve the Lord, denying the work of the Holy Spirit within you.

Your new heart can become tainted by wrong desires, when you set your mind on fleshly things. When you are willing to turn back to the Lord, to embrace His best purposes for you, like David you will want to pray, 'Create in me a pure heart, O God, and renew a steadfast spirit within me' (Ps. 51:10).

When you turn to Him with renewed repentance, He releases afresh within you the power of His Holy Spirit. Once again you feel clean before Him and your desire to walk in His ways is restored.

'But we have the mind of Christ' (1 Cor. 2:16). The Holy Spirit wants to inform your mind of God's mind, so that you think according to His ways rather than your own natural ways. Because your mind has been conditioned to think naturally and even negatively, opposing the Word of God, it takes time for your thinking to be renewed. And what you think determines what you do. This is why Paul says 'those who live in accordance with the Spirit have their minds set on what the Spirit desires' (Rom. 8:5).

We have the warning of Scripture not to lean on our own understanding. We need to realise that God's thoughts might differ totally from our thoughts, but that His thoughts are higher than ours. His thoughts are truth.

Our bodies try to distract us from God's purpose by making us aware of their desire for gratification. We know conflict between the spirit and the flesh, but we have God's promise that He will never allow us to be tempted beyond what we can endure. The Lord is in the centre of such conflict with you because His Spirit is within you. It is His life within you that is to fight against the world, the flesh and the devil. '. . . the one who is in you is greater than the one who is in the world' (1 John 4:4).

When Jesus spoke of the Holy Spirit, He also said that rivers of living water would flow out from your innermost being, from out of your heart. 'By this he meant the Spirit, whom those who believed in him were later to receive. Up to that time the Spirit had not been given, since Jesus had not yet been glorified' (John 7:39).

Now that Jesus has been glorified, and His Spirit has been poured out, many rivers can flow from your heart. The rivers are not rivers of negative thinking and critical speech, but of praise to God, of faith in what He has done, and of love towards others.

The positive life of God's Spirit within you is greater than all the negatives around you. God is far greater than Satan. The Spirit is more powerful than the flesh. Jesus has overcome the world. So hear the Lord speaking His words into your heart to encourage your faith.

---

### Meditation:
THE ONE WHO IS IN YOU IS GREATER THAN THE ONE WHO IS IN THE WORLD (1 JOHN 4:4).

The mind controlled by the Spirit is life and peace (ROM. 8:6).

Live by the Spirit, and you will not gratify the desires of the sinful nature (GAL. 5:16).

### Praise:
Surely the righteous will praise your name and the upright will live before you (PS. 140:13).

# 42. *The Spirit within Me*

'For God did not give us a spirit of timidity but a spirit of power, of love and of self-discipline' (2 TIM. 1:7).

Lord, give me boldness by your Holy Spirit, please.

**READING:** 2 TIMOTHY. 1:6–9
I remind you to fan into flame the gift of God, which is in you through the laying on of my hands. For God did not give us a spirit of timidity, but a spirit of power, of love and of self-discipline.

So do not be ashamed to testify about our Lord, or ashamed of me his prisoner. But join with me in suffering for the gospel, by the power of God, who has saved us and called us to a holy life – not because of anything we have done but because of his own purpose and grace.

---

If you are to speak the truth about yourself as someone with a new heart and in whom God has put His Spirit, you need to say:

I have a spirit of power;
I have a spirit of love;
I have a spirit of self-discipline.

You can never say truthfully that you lack the resources to share God's love and power with others.

Jesus promised: 'But you will receive power when the Holy Spirit comes on you; and you will be my witnesses in Jerusalem, and in all Judea and Samaria, and to the ends of the earth' (Acts 1:8). Because you have received the Holy Spirit the power of God is within you. You do not have to be afraid because his presence is within you and His power is available to you. That power is greater than any worldly or demonic power. It is God's power, which will enable you to do anything He asks of you.

*You have a spirit of power – God's power.* Jesus prayed that 'the love you have for me may be in them and that I myself may be in them' (John 17:26). This prayer was fulfilled in you when you received the Holy Spirit. You have the love of the Father and the Son within you. This demonstrates the immensity of His love for you and His desire for this love to be expressed through you. *You have a spirit of love* – not of fear or hate or lust, which are all opposites of love.

Self-discipline is part of the fruit of the Holy Spirit (Gal. 5:23), one of the qualities He produces in the believer. The Amplified Bible translates this as having a 'well balanced mind and discipline and self-control'. You are able to be in control of your thinking and do not have to receive the fearful, negative, accusing, condemning thoughts that the enemy wants to plant in your mind. If you think correctly, you will act in accordance with God's will. *You have a spirit of self-discipline*, a sound mind.

Your mind is not to be a plaything of the enemy. This is his first line of attack. Yes, he knows that if he can encourage you to think incorrectly then you will also speak and act incorrectly. By contrast, the Holy Spirit informs your mind of God's thoughts, reminding you of His Words. In every situation He wants you to be attentive to His voice. It is so important, therefore, to receive His Words and to store them within your heart.

You can live in freedom from fear; Jesus is with you always. He lives in you and you live in Him. In Him there is no fear. He loves you and His perfect love casts out all fear (1 John 4:18). Praise Him that He has given you a spirit of power, love and self-discipline. Your life does not need to be dominated by negative thoughts or feelings. Your trust is in Him who loves you perfectly.

**Meditation:**
FOR GOD DID NOT GIVE US A SPIRIT OF
TIMIDITY, BUT A SPIRIT OF POWER, OF
LOVE AND OF SELF-DISCIPLINE (2 TIM.
1:7).

But you will receive power when the Holy Spirit
comes on you (ACTS 1:8).

Do not be afraid . . . You are my witnesses (ISA. 44:8).

**Praise:**
God is our refuge and strength, an ever present help in
trouble. Therefore we will not fear, though the earth
give way and the mountains fall into the heart of the
sea (PS. 46:1–2).

# 43. Heart, Mind and Body

'You, however, are controlled not by the sinful nature but by
the Spirit, if the Spirit of God lives in you' (ROM. 8:9).

Holy Spirit, I want to walk in your ways, not those of the
flesh.

**READING:** ROMANS 12:1–2
Therefore, I urge you, brothers, in view of God's
mercy, to offer your bodies as living sacrifices, holy
and pleasing to God – which is your spiritual worship.
Do not conform any longer to the pattern of this
world, but be transformed by the renewing of your
mind. Then you will be able to test and approve what
God's will is – his good, pleasing and perfect will.

The Lord wants to produce in your life all the ninefold fruit of the Spirit. As you allow the Holy Spirit freedom in your life, He will produce in you the fruit of love, joy, peace, patience, kindness, goodness, faithfulness, gentleness and self-control. He will release His power and healing in your life. From you will flow rivers of love towards others as you seek to serve them in the name of Jesus.

Your body is to express the new life He has put within you. It is not enough to possess the Holy Spirit; God wants to see His life expressed in your life. He has made you holy in His sight, so you are to offer your body to Him as a living sacrifice. This is the worship He desires: a body offered to Him to express His holy life. He is renewing your thinking so that you know what His perfect will is, and He is empowering you with His Spirit to enable you to do it.

The ways of the world are often at odds with the ways of God. Every day you will have to make decisions as to whether you will act in ways the world admires, pleasing the flesh and honouring the devil, or whether you will choose to deny self and follow Jesus.

There is nothing wrong with the new heart God has given you. As you use your mind and mouth correctly, you can begin to express the abundance that God has put in your heart in positive action. You can stop using your mouth in ways which deny the truth of God's Spirit within you. God will transform your thinking and speaking.

To be always submitted in these ways involves the daily offering of yourselves to Him. 'Finally, brothers, whatever is true, whatever is noble, whatever is right, whatever is pure, whatever is lovely, whatever is admirable – if anything is excellent or praiseworthy – think about such things. Whatever you have learned or received or heard from me, or seen in me – put it into practice. And the God of peace will be with you' (Phil. 4:8–9).

As you use your mind in the right way, so you will then act in the right way. Your bodily appetites will not rule you. Your new heart will rule the mind, and the mind the body. In this way the reign of Jesus, who is your Lord, will be expressed in your life. You will do what He wants you to do.

Receiving the Word of God is vital to this whole process. The Holy Spirit working in your heart witnesses to the truth of the Word. Your mind absorbs the Word and your will translates it into action.

The secret is not to concentrate on the flesh and try to fight it, but to concentrate on the Lord Jesus and pray that the Holy Spirit will keep you in His ways. When you are pleasing the Lord, the flesh has no room to express itself.

Jesus wants to speak personally to you, encouraging you not only to receive the Holy Spirit, but to live by the Spirit. God wants every part of you, spirit, soul and body, to express His life which is within you.

---

**Meditation:**
LIVE BY THE SPIRIT, AND YOU WILL NOT GRATIFY THE DESIRES OF THE SINFUL NATURE (GAL. 5:16).

Pursue righteousness, faith, love and peace, along with those who call on the Lord out of a pure heart (2 TIM. 2:22).

The grace of our Lord was poured out on me abundantly, along with the faith and love that are in Christ Jesus (1 TIM. 1:14).


**Praise:**
Your ways, O God, are holy. What god is so great as our God? (PS. 77:13).

# 44. Loving Obedience

'If you love me, you will obey what I command' (JOHN 14:15).

Lord Jesus, I want to show my love for you by obeying you.

### READING: LUKE 6:46–9
Why do you call me, 'Lord, Lord,' and do not do what I say? I will show you what he is like who comes to me and hears my words and puts them into practice. He is like a man building a house, who dug down deep and laid the foundation on rock. When the flood came, the torrent struck that house but could not shake it, because it was well built. But the one who hears my words and does not put them into practice is like a man who built a house on the ground without a foundation. The moment the torrent struck that house, it collapsed and its destruction was complete.

---

It is easy to imagine these two houses in the midst of a violent storm. One withstands the might of the wind and rain; the other is swept away, its collapse and destruction complete. The first is built on rock, the other on sand, without a foundation.

Those who build on the rock are those who hear the words of Jesus *and put them into practice*. It is not enough to hear the Word; we are to live the Word. It is worth digging deeply to ensure your life is based on the solid rock of God's Word.

The man who builds on sand also hears the words of Jesus, but does not put them into practice. Because he is not practising the Word he cannot withstand the storms of life.

Through this method of prayer, and in other ways, God speaks His words to our hearts. Faith comes from hearing those words *and is expressed in acting upon them*. We are to be not only doers, but doers of the Word.

Jesus points us to the absolute security to be found in obeying what He says. Obedience is an outworking of our love for the Lord. 'Whoever has my commands and obeys them, he is the one who loves me. He who loves me will be loved by my Father, and I too will love him and show myself to him' (John 14:21).

The rewards for obedience are amazing: 'Jesus replied, "If anyone loves me, he will obey my teaching. My Father will love him, and we will come to him and make our home with him"' (John 14:23). The message is clear. Jesus does not ask us simply to agree with His teaching, but to live it as an outworking of our love for Him.

Our love for Jesus, and our obedience to Him, is a response to His amazing love for us. It is impossible to express adequately in words the nature of that love. We can only experience it continually and increasingly, and be grateful for it. The knowledge of that love is like rock beneath our feet.

As Christians it is our desire to express God's love to others every day of our lives. We do this in our relationships, our acceptance and forgiveness of others; we do this in the ways we serve and encourage people. All this is like living on rock, for it is living His Word. To love one another, as He has loved us is building on rock; to hear that but to live a life of hatred, lust, greed and selfishness is building on sand.

To live by faith is to build on rock. To speak and live as one who is in Christ is to build on rock. To put the resources of God's kingdom to work in your life is to build on rock. To appropriate His promises is to build on rock. To resist the devil and all his works is to build on rock. For these are all ways of putting the Word into practice.

When you depend on yourself instead of the Lord, it is like stepping on to sand. You may know and believe the Word, but are not practising it at that point. The same is true when you speak negatively, think of yourself outside of Christ, look to men and natural resources instead of the Lord and His heavenly resources. It is also like walking on sand when you disbelieve the promises God gives you, and allow the devil to trample all over you.

Make sure your house is built on rock so that you live on the

rock, and don't step out of His provision on to shifting sand.
Know that the Father and Son have come to make their home
with you.

---

**Meditation:**
IF YOU LOVE ME, YOU WILL OBEY
WHAT I COMMAND (JOHN 14:15).

Whoever has my commands and obeys them, he is the
one who loves me (JOHN 14:21).

He who loves me will be loved by my Father, and I too
will love him and show myself to him (JOHN 14:21).

**Praise:**
He set my feet on a rock and gave me a firm place to
stand (PS. 40:2).

# 45. *The Fruit of the Spirit is . . . Joy*

'But the angel said to them, "Do not be afraid. I bring you
good news of great joy that will be for all the people"' (LUKE
2:10).

Holy Spirit, please fill me with joy.

### READING: JOHN 16:20-4
I tell you the truth, you will weep and mourn while the
world rejoices. You will grieve, but your grief will
turn to joy. A woman giving birth to a child has pain
because her time has come; but when her baby is born

she forgets the anguish because of her joy that a child is born into the world. So with you: Now is your time of grief, but I will see you again and you will rejoice, and no-one will take away your joy. In that day you will no longer ask me anything. I tell you the truth, my Father will give you whatever you ask in my name. Until now you have not asked for anything in my name. Ask and you will receive, and your joy will be complete.

---

Because God is love, the first-fruit of the Holy Spirit is love. He is the Spirit of love living within you and wanting to guide you in loving obedience. However, the Spirit will produce other fruit in you as well.

Jesus was a man of joy. When God describes His own Son, He says: 'You have loved righteousness and hated wickedness; therefore God, your God, has set you above your companions by anointing you with the oil of joy' (Heb. 1:9). The righteous life is a joyful life.

Sometimes Christians appear very dour and sombre, without conveying the joy which comes from knowing Jesus. God intends your joy to be full. 'Ask and you will receive, and your joy will be complete' (John 16:24).

Jesus tells us to live in His love so we can be full of joy. 'I have told you this so that my joy may be in you and that your joy may be complete' (John 15:11). No one can take from you the joy of knowing the risen Christ; 'no-one will take away your joy' (John 16:22).

Because joy is part of the fruit of the Holy Spirit God has put in you, He wants to see this joy expressed in your life. Just as God's love is not based on emotion, although it is bound to touch your emotions, so with His joy. We are speaking of the joy of the Spirit, who is constantly within you no matter what your feelings and circumstances. It is this joy that no man, no situation, no demonic force can take from you. You have this joy whether you feel joyful or not.

God calls you to a life of faith, and joy is the barometer of your faith. A person cannot be in a position of faith without being joyful. Your situation may appear to be completely hopeless, but the joy of the Lord is your strength! You know He is present with you; you know He will never leave you or forsake you. You know He hears your cry for help and answers you – even though there may not be any immediate evidence of that.

Even repentance can be joyful, not that we enjoy confessing our sins, but because turning away from sin and back to Him leads to a fresh revelation of His love.

Jesus was 'full of joy through the Holy Spirit' (Luke 10:21), and that is God's purpose for you. Express that joy in praise and worship, in loving and serving others, in giving to God and others with a joyful heart.

---

**Meditation:**
I HAVE TOLD YOU THIS SO THAT MY JOY MAY BE IN YOU AND THAT YOUR JOY MAY BE COMPLETE (JOHN 15:11).

No-one will take away your joy (JOHN 16:22).

Those on the rock are the ones who receive the word with joy when they hear it (LUKE 8:13).

**Praise:**
You have made known to me the path of life; you will fill me with joy in your presence (PS. 16:11).

# 46. The Fruit of the Spirit is . . . Peace

'And the peace of God, which transcends all understanding, will guard your hearts and your minds in Christ Jesus' (PHIL. 4:7).

Jesus, you are my peace.

> **READING:** JOHN 14:26–7
> But the Counsellor, the Holy Spirit, whom the Father will send in my name, will teach you all things and will remind you of everything I have said to you. Peace I leave with you; my peace I give you. I do not give to you as the world gives. Do not let your hearts be troubled and do not be afraid.

---

Jesus stood among the disciples in His risen body and gave them His peace. 'Peace be with you,' He said (John 20:19). This fulfilled the promise He had given them earlier. These words are not simply a greeting, they convey His peace to His disciples, who at the time were in a fearful state.

God's peace is different from the world's idea of peace. People think of peace being the absence of war, or the lack of noise when the children have gone to bed. But God's peace is part of the fruit of the Spirit because 'he himself is our peace' (Eph. 2:14). It is a positive gift from God to His children.

Paul describes this peace as being beyond our understanding. 'And the peace of God, which transcends all understanding, will guard your hearts and your minds in Christ Jesus' (Phil. 4:7). You receive this peace in three dimensions.

First, you are at peace with God, which means there is a sense of well-being between the Lord and yourself. There is no conviction of sin because you know you are cleansed and forgiven. You can experience this peace because Jesus has made 'peace through his blood, shed on the cross' (Col. 1:20).

Second, you can be at peace with others: 'Let the peace of Christ rule in your hearts, since as members of one body you were called to peace. And be thankful' (Col. 3:15). Your peace with God is expressed in your unity and peace with others. 'Live in peace with each other' (1 Thess. 5:13).

Third, because you are at peace with God and others you have peace within yourself. 'Now may the Lord of peace himself give you peace at all times and in every way' (2 Thess. 3:16).

The Lord gives this peace through the activity of His Spirit within you. 'May God himself, the God of peace, sanctify you through and through. May your whole spirit, soul and body be kept blameless at the coming of our Lord Jesus Christ' (1 Thess. 5:23).

You will know His peace as you follow the leading of His Spirit. When you walk in the flesh, you lose your peace with God; you are not at peace with yourself and it is not long before your relationships with others begin to be affected. When you are at peace with the Lord you have the sense of well-being, even in the middle of what appears to be turmoil and confusion, for that peace comes from your heavenly circumstances not your earthly ones.

Whenever you feel anxious and are distracted by your situation use this sentence in meditation. Sit down quietly and receive the peace of God, for Jesus is with you, speaking His words of peace. Remember, these are not words about peace, but words which convey His peace to you.

---

**Meditation:**
PEACE I LEAVE WITH YOU; MY PEACE I GIVE YOU (JOHN 14:27).

Peace be with you! (JOHN 20:19).

Now may the Lord of peace himself give you peace at all times and in every way (2 THESS. 3:16).

**Praise:**
My soul finds rest in God alone (PS. 62:1).

# 47. The Fruit of the Spirit is . . . Patience

'Love is patient' (1 COR. 13:4).

Holy Spirit, produce the fruit of patience in me, please.

**READING:** COLOSSIANS 1:10–14
And we pray this in order that you may live a life worthy of the Lord and may please him in every way: bearing fruit in every good work, growing in the knowledge of God, being strengthened with all power according to his glorious might so that you may have great endurance and patience, and joyfully giving thanks to the Father, who has qualified you to share in the inheritance of the saints in the kingdom of light. For he has rescued us from the dominion of darkness and brought us into the kingdom of the Son he loves, in whom we have redemption, the forgiveness of sins.

---

The Lord is infinitely patient with us. It is an aspect of His character and therefore part of the personality of the Holy Spirit. So He wants to produce the fruit of patience in you.

Many recognise their need for more patience. In public they usually manage to control themselves and their tempers. In private they relax their guard and take out their frustrations and disappointments on those they love most, on husband or wife and children. This causes them distress because they do not want to hurt those who are most precious to them.

'Love is patient,' says Paul. In love a husband or wife learns to put up with the failings of his or her partner and the constant demands of the children. It is an expression of their love. But we all recognise the limitations of our human love and therefore our human patience. We recognise the need to avail ourselves of the Lord's resources, of the patience which comes by the Spirit.

'Lord, give me patience – but hurry' is a common joke, but expresses something which is often true in our attitudes.

Fruit takes time to grow. The more conscious you are of God's love at work in you, the more the fruit of patience will be evident in your life. It is not a matter of simply asking God for patience. Because this comes as part of the fruit of the Spirit working within you, it will grow alongside other aspects of the Spirit's activity within you.

Abraham inherited the promises of God by faith with patience. It is that patience which is so often lacking with us. We would like instantaneous answers to every prayer. The Holy Spirit helps us to maintain our faith position until we see the promises fulfilled.

We are to be patient in the face of adversity, patient with those who scoff at us because we believe, with those who cannot understand the gospel because they are bound by unbelief.

We are to be patient as we await the return of Jesus in glory and triumph.

And we are to be patient with one another, expressing the love of Jesus to one another in forgiveness and encouragement. 'But for that very reason I was shown mercy so that in me, the worst of sinners, Christ Jesus might display his unlimited patience as an example for those who would believe on him and receive eternal life' (1 Tim. 1:16).

Hear the Lord encouraging you now. The Spirit desires to create in you the humility, gentleness and patience of which these words speak.

---

**Meditation:**
BE COMPLETELY HUMBLE AND GEN-
TLE; BE PATIENT, BEARING WITH ONE
ANOTHER IN LOVE (EPH. 4:2).

Love is patient (1 COR. 13:4).

He is patient with you (2 PET. 3:9).

Be patient with everyone (1 THESS. 5:14).

**Praise:**
I waited patiently for the Lord; he turned to me and heard my cry (PS. 40:1).

# 48.  *The Fruit of the Spirit is . . . Kindness*

'Love is kind' (1 COR. 13:4).

Jesus, I want to express your kindness through the Holy Spirit working in me.

### READING: EPHESIANS 2:4–10
But because of His great love for us, God, who is rich in mercy, made us alive with Christ even when we were dead in transgressions – it is by grace you have been saved. And God raised us up with Christ and seated us with him in the heavenly realms in Christ Jesus, in order that in the coming ages he might show the incomparable riches of his grace, expressed in his kindness to us in Christ Jesus. For it is by grace you have been saved, through faith – and this not from yourselves, it is the gift of God – not by works, so that no-one can boast. For we are God's workmanship, created in Christ Jesus to do good works, which God prepared in advance for us to do.

---

All the fruits of the Spirit abound in Jesus's life. His kindness is shown in the loving way He dealt with those in need, in His willingness to forgive the disciples regularly for their unbelief, in His patience with them in all their failures.

And so the Holy Spirit wants to reproduce His kindness in us. We are told to 'Be kind and compassionate to one another, forgiving each other, just as in Christ God forgave you' (Eph. 4:32). Paul also says, '. . . always try to be kind to each other and to everyone else' (1 Thess. 5:15). 'And the Lord's servant . . . must be kind to everyone' he says (2 Tim. 2:24). We are to clothe ourselves with kindness (Col. 3:12).

Of course it is easier to be kind to those you find easy to love. But your call is to love all your Christian brethren, and your neighbour as yourself. God's intention is that you express kindness to all, which is easier said than done!

The quality of Christian witness suffers seriously when kindness is lacking in relationships. None of us is perfect in our expression of Jesus's love, but Christians too often deal with one another in thoughtless and unloving ways, thinking little of the consequences of their words and actions and their effects upon others. This results in hurt and sometimes deep bitterness, and is the consequence of fleshly decisions and actions rather than those filled with Holy Spirit activity.

Jesus needed to be stern at times, even with the disciples. But He was never unkind. He reflected the fact that God's anger is tempered by mercy and grace. He confronted the Pharisees and others with their hypocrisy; yet loving kindness awaited those who turned to Him.

Love is often expressed in acts of positive kindness – in not dealing with people as they deserve, but with graciousness, love and mercy. It helps to remember the ways in which God has expressed His kindness to you. This will help motivate you to be kind to others, depending not on yourself, but on the resources of God's Spirit within you.

The kingdom principle applies once again: The measure you give is the measure you get back. 'A kind man benefits himself, but a cruel man brings himself harm' (Prov. 11:17). Never forget, kindness is the fruit of God's Spirit working within you to express the life of Jesus through you. The more the Spirit abounds in your life, the more that kindness will be manifested.

As you receive God's Word, believe the Spirit is working within you to enable you to clothe yourself with kindness in your dealings with others.

---

**Meditation:**
CLOTHE YOURSELVES WITH . . . KIND-NESS (COL. 3:12).

Love is kind (1 COR. 13:4).

Be kind and compassionate to one another, forgiving each other, just as in Christ God forgave you (EPH. 4:32).

**Praise:**
He shows unfailing kindness to his anointed (PS. 18:50).

# 49. The Fruit of the Spirit is . . . Goodness

'"Why do you call me good?" Jesus answered. "No-one is good – except God alone"' (MARK 10:18).

Holy Spirit, help me at all times to do what is good.

**READING:** LUKE 6:43–5
No good tree bears bad fruit, nor does a bad tree bear good fruit. Each tree is recognised by its own fruit. People do not pick figs from thorn-bushes, or grapes from briers. The good man brings good things out of the good stored up in his heart, and the evil man brings evil things out of the evil stored up in his heart. For out of the overflow of his heart his mouth speaks.

---

Paul gives a clear description of man in his natural state: 'There is no-one righteous, not even one; there is no-one who understands, no-one who seeks God. All have turned away, they have together become worthless' (Rom. 3:10–12). No one is good in himself, no matter how many 'good works' he accomplishes. Everyone is born with a rebellious spirit and desires naturally to walk in his own ways. God alone is good, says Jesus (Mark 10:18).

This conflicts with modern rational thinking, in which man is thought to be good in himself. So many people think of themselves as living 'good' lives, by which they mean that they are law-abiding citizens who do not harm others and may even seek to help them.

This fails to take into account the fact of sin. Even those who try to lead 'good' lives sin regularly against the Lord. Without a Saviour their sin renders them unacceptable to God. Even if it seems many of their actions would please Him, they themselves can only please the Holy God when washed of their sins and made holy in His sight.

The blood of Jesus cleanses us from the things which are not good in God's eyes and the Holy Spirit creates in us what is good. Jesus reflected perfectly His Father's goodness. He, in turn, wants you to reflect His goodness. But this is not some inherent goodness you have within yourself, but the goodness which comes from the Holy Spirit's activity within you.

Before conversion, your spiritual heart was diseased; when you were born again the Lord gave you a new heart. It does not matter how bad the tree was beforehand, God makes you a new creation, a new tree, a good tree, able to bear good fruit.

John the Baptist told people to prove their repentance by the fruit they produced in their lives. Jesus says something similar; a good tree cannot bear bad fruit; a bad tree cannot bear good fruit.

This does not mean you are to strive in your own strength to be good. The tree produces fruit as a result of the life-producing sap flowing through its branches. The goodness God wants to see in your life flows from the sap of the Holy Spirit producing the positive works of goodness and love within you. He prompts you to do what is good and right in each situation, but also supplies the ability to do it.

You want to do what is best for those you love. This will require correction and discipline at times; but mainly it is a question of giving to them, because their good is your concern. Such goodness is to flow out of you as a river of living water towards all around you; seeking the good and welfare of others, expressing God's goodness to them. You will have the right motivation to obey the leading of the Spirit to do this if you remain aware of His constant goodness towards you.

Goodness is expressed in the moral choices you make, as well as in your willingness to serve others. Because you are a child of His kingdom, He wants the life of this kingdom to be evidenced in the choices you make, because you live by the principles of the kingdom, which are always good. You cannot reflect the life of the king or His kingdom through making wrong choices.

Goodness is to be shown to all, even to those who hate you, because you are Jesus's witness wherever you are, regardless of what is happening to you. As you receive His words today, remember that the Lord supplies all the grace you need to accomplish what He asks of you.

---

**Meditation:**
TRUST IN THE LORD AND DO GOOD (PS. 37:3).

The Lord is good to all (PS. 145:9).

He satisfies my desires with good things (PS. 103:5).

**Praise:**
I will extol the Lord at all times; his praise will always be on my lips (PS. 34:1).

# 50. The Fruit of the Spirit is . . . Faithfulness

'I will betroth you in faithfulness, and you will acknowledge the Lord' (HOS. 2:20).

Holy Spirit, please keep me faithful.

**READING:** PSALM 89:1–8
I will sing of the Lord's great love for ever; with my mouth I will make your faithfulness known through all generations. I will declare that your love stands firm for ever, that you established your faithfulness in heaven itself.

You said, 'I have made a covenant with my chosen one, I have sworn to David my servant, I will establish your line forever and make your throne firm through all generations.'

The heavens praise your wonders, O Lord, your faithfulness too, in the assembly of the holy ones. For who in the skies above can compare with the Lord? Who is like the Lord among the heavenly beings? In the council of the holy ones God is greatly feared; he is more awesome than all who surround him. O Lord God Almighty, who is like you? You are mighty, O Lord, and your faithfulness surrounds you.

---

God is always faithful. He will never fail His children. He will never deny Himself by acting unfaithfully. He will always honour His Word; He watches over it to see it fulfilled. He is always ready to honour His covenant promises to those who belong to Him.

Because faithfulness is an essential part of His being, He wants the Holy Spirit to reproduce that faithfulness in you.

The word faithful can mean two things. First, it involves being full of faith, full of trust and confidence in God's Word, in His love and faithfulness. God is so faithful to His Word, His Spirit will constantly direct you to that Word.

Second, faithful means to remain true to the Lord, reflecting His own faithfulness. The Bible is full of statements concerning God's faithfulness. 'You are mighty, O Lord, and your faithfulness surrounds you' (Ps. 89:8). Later in the same Psalm we read, 'but I will not take my love from him, nor will I ever betray my faithfulness' (v.33).

Paul makes it clear that our lack of faith cannot 'nullify God's faithfulness' (Rom. 3:3). He will always remain faithful, even if His children are not always faithful. But He rewards those who do remain faithful to Him. 'Be faithful, even to the point of death, and I will give you the crown of life' (Rev. 2:10).

The enemy tries to encourage God's children to fear they would not be faithful if their faith was to be subjected to some serious trial. However, God always gives grace as and when it is needed. Faithfulness is a work of the Holy Spirit within your life. He will not leave you to your own devices, and is always ready to help whenever you turn to Him and trust in Him. It is His purpose to keep you faithful to the end, and He will do it. 'May God himself, the God of peace, sanctify you through and through. May your whole spirit, soul and body be kept blameless at the coming of our Lord Jesus Christ. The one who calls you is faithful and he will do it' (1 Thess. 5:23–4).

When you appreciate this truth, you will be liberated from the constant temptation to strive. You will never prove faithful by your own efforts; only by the precious work of the Holy Spirit within you. You can be faithful only because He is faithful, and is ready to produce the fruit of faithfulness within you. 'The Lord is faithful to all his promises and loving towards all he has made' (Ps. 145:13).

The Spirit is ready to lead and guide you in the way God wants you to go. He prompts you to co-operate with Him by making the decisions pleasing to Him. Even when you fail to hear and obey Him, He remains faithful to you because of His commitment to you as your Father. When you confess your sins He is faithful to the atoning work of Jesus and forgives your sins, cleansing you from all unrighteousness.

Whichever way you turn, the Lord is there in His faithful love, wanting to give to you and encourage you. Even when you go through the greatest times of testing, He will never fail in His love for you. Neither does He want you to fail in your faithfulness to Him. Your faithfulness is a response to His faithfulness.

Hear Jesus speaking these words to your heart. Once they become part of you, they will be a constant source of encouragement to you.

---

**Meditation:**
I WILL NEVER LEAVE YOU NOR FORSAKE YOU (JOSH. 1:5).

Be faithful . . . and I will give you the crown of life (REV. 2:10).

The faithfulness of the Lord endures for ever (PS. 117:2).

**Praise:**
His compassions never fail. They are new every morning; great is your faithfulness (LAM. 3:22–3).

# 51. The Fruit of the Spirit is . . . Gentleness

'Let your gentleness be evident to all. The Lord is near' (PHIL. 4:5).

Lord Jesus, I can only be gentle through your grace.

**READING:** MATTHEW 11:28–30
Come to me, all you who are weary and burdened, and I will give you rest. Take my yoke upon you and learn from me, for I am gentle and humble in heart, and you will find rest for your souls. For my yoke is easy and my burden is light.

---

Perhaps gentleness is the most misunderstood part of the Holy Spirit's fruit. People often associate gentleness with weakness. Yet Jesus Himself said that He was gentle, and you could not accuse Him of weakness.

We are to be completely humble and gentle (Eph. 4:2); and let our gentleness be evident to all (Phil. 4:5). So this is a quality the Lord wants to see in all His children. Indeed, it is His desire to see every part of the fruit of the Spirit reproduced in the lives of all who belong to Him.

Notice the way gentleness and being humble are linked together by both Jesus and Paul. Jesus described Himself as gentle and humble in heart. When He rode in triumph into Jerusalem He was 'gentle and riding on a donkey' (Matt. 21:5). Paul says, 'Be completely humble and gentle' (Eph. 4:2).

Pride causes a strident harshness in people's lives, and therefore in their dealings with others. There is great strength in humility. Jesus came as the servant of all, but He was the man of authority and power. It is not weak to be humble and gentle.

Gentleness is another aspect of love. Love 'does not boast, it is not proud' (1 Cor. 13:4). There is a gentleness about love, a desire to protect those loved from harm.

The Lord disciplines us in His love, but He does not do so harshly. He does not lord it over us in a worldly way. Because of His great love for us He is exceedingly gentle, pointing us in the right direction, prompting us to obey His will, giving time for repentance, but never forcing us into a begrudging obedience. That is an expression of His gentle and humble heart.

And so He desires that we treat others similarly. Instead of being resentful we are to forgive. When a brother sins we are to try and restore him. We are to encourage one another, not judge and condemn.

These things are not possible when there is no love. The Spirit produces gentleness as an expression of God's love in our lives. When you express His love, you will be gentle with others. As with other aspects of His life, you will find it easier to show gentleness towards others by being consistently thankful of God's gentleness with you. 'In everything, do to others what you would have them do to you' says Jesus (Matt. 7:12). This becomes possible when you know you can do for others what God has already done for you!

**Meditation:**
I AM GENTLE AND HUMBLE IN HEART (MATT. 11:29).

Be completely humble and gentle (EPH. 4:2).

Let your gentleness be evident to all. The Lord is near (PHIL. 4:5).

**Praise:**
For the Lord takes delight in his people; he crowns the humble with salvation (PS. 149:4).

# 52. The Fruit of the Spirit is . . . Self-control

'Therefore, prepare your minds for action; be self-controlled; set your hope fully on the grace to be given you when Jesus Christ is revealed' (1 PET. 1:13).

Holy Spirit, help me to be self-controlled at all times.

**READING:** 1 THESSALONIANS 5:5–11

You are all sons of the light and sons of the day. We do not belong to the night or to the darkness. So then, let us not be like others, who are asleep, but let us be alert and self-controlled. For those who sleep, sleep at night, and those who get drunk, get drunk at night. But since we belong to the day, let us be self-controlled, putting on faith and love as a breastplate, and the hope of salvation as a helmet. For God did not appoint us to suffer wrath but to receive salvation through our Lord Jesus Christ. He died for us so that, whether we are awake or asleep, we may live together with him. Therefore encourage one another and build each other up, just as in fact you are doing.

---

Selfishness and self-seeking lead to a lack of self-control. Expressing the 'self' life, the life of the flesh, opposes the work of the Spirit within us. The Holy Spirit wants to keep that self life under control. Love 'is not self-seeking' (1 Cor. 13:5). So the Spirit sounds warning bells within us when we are in danger of grieving the Lord.

God lives within you to express His life through you. If the things that self desires oppose the purposes of God, those selfish impulses have to be denied. Then the life of His Spirit can flow readily through your life.

Peter warns: 'Be self-controlled and alert. Your enemy the devil prowls around like a roaring lion looking for someone to devour. Resist him, standing firm in the faith' (1 Pet. 5:8–9). The enemy wants to stir up all the wrong desires, motives and intentions. He wants you to act in ways that are unloving and which oppose the Spirit. The Lord, on the other hand, wants to produce the qualities of Jesus in you by the power of the Holy Spirit, bringing your spirit, soul and body willingly and lovingly under His control.

The devil inspires hatred, selfishness and greed; the Spirit produces love. The enemy wants you to be joyless, complaining, morose, defeated and dejected: the Holy Spirit gives you joy. Satan wants to create tension, anxiety and disunity; the Spirit produces peace in you. The enemy wants you to judge and criticise; the Spirit wants you to be kind.

The devil tempts you to selfishness and self-gratification; the Holy Spirit gives you the ability to be self-controlled, to deny the attempts of the world, the flesh and the devil to lead you away from the purposes of God.

As you receive God's Word, He encourages you to put on faith and love as a breastplate. God is working within you by His Spirit to keep the self life under control and enable that love and faith to be a defence for you.

---

### Meditation:
LET US BE SELF-CONTROLLED, PUTTING ON FAITH AND LOVE AS A BREASTPLATE (1 THESS. 5:8).

Love . . . is not self-seeking (1 COR. 13:4–5).

You, however, are controlled . . . by the Spirit, if the Spirit of God lives in you (ROM. 8:9).

### Praise:
The Lord reigns, let the earth be glad (PS. 97:1).

# PART SIX

# YOUR LIFE IN THE KINGDOM

# 53. The Kingdom of God

'Do not be afraid, little flock, for your Father has been pleased to give you the kingdom' (LUKE 12:32).

Lord, I need to have the revelation that the kingdom is within me.

**READING:** LUKE 17:20–1
Once, having been asked by the Pharisees when the kingdom of God would come, Jesus replied, 'The kingdom of God does not come visibly, nor will people say, "Here it is," or "There it is," because the kingdom of God is within you.'

---

When Jesus began to teach and preach, He had a simple proclamation: 'Repent, for the kingdom of heaven is near' (Matt. 4:17). The king of heaven had come to dwell among men and brought His kingdom within their reach. When they submitted their lives to Him, they came under His rule and reign. At the same time all the riches and resources of this kingdom became their inheritance, an inheritance which they can begin to appropriate immediately.

When Jesus reigns in your life you are not only part of His kingdom, you possess the kingdom of God or the kingdom of heaven. This is not a visible kingdom. You cannot say it is over here or over there: it is within you.

When you put your faith in Jesus, God gave you the gift of His kingdom. In His many parables Jesus teaches about the nature of this kingdom. It is like a tiny mustard seed which, when fully grown, becomes a tree that birds can nest in. Contained within that seed is all that will potentially grow from it, just as everything the oak tree becomes is contained potentially in the acorn. All the seed needs is the right soil and water, in order to grow to fruitfulness.

The Lord has planted the seed of His kingdom in your heart and life. All the life and resources of that kingdom are yours potentially. Your life is to be good soil that will produce thirtyfold, sixtyfold, or a hundred times what was sown. He has watered that seed with the power of the Holy Spirit – God living within you to enable you to live as a child of the kingdom.

So the kingdom is not something you are given when you die if you prove worthy enough to receive it. God has already given you this gift because of the worthiness of Jesus. You have the life of the kingdom within you. The Holy Spirit enables you to live as a child of God's kingdom, enjoying the privileges, but also facing the responsibilities of such a position.

When you die and go to be with the Lord, you will know the fullness of the kingdom. Until then, He wants to see you appropriating His riches, and expressing the life of His kingdom in your life. He teaches you to pray, 'your kingdom come, your will be done on earth as it is in heaven' (Matt. 6:10). He tells you to seek first the kingdom and His righteousness and you will not need to be anxious about anything. For the king of heaven is the king of love and He cares perfectly for those who are His subjects.

Because His kingdom is within you, He wants you to be subject to Him in all things so that nothing can hinder the flow of His kingdom life through you. Receive this revelation in your heart, for it is the revelation Jesus came to give you.

---

**Meditation:**
THE KINGDOM OF GOD IS WITHIN YOU (LUKE 17:21).

But seek first his kingdom and his righteousness, and all these things will be given to you as well (MATT. 6:33).

Your kingdom come, your will be done on earth as it is in heaven (MATT. 6:10).

**Praise:**
They will tell of the glory of your kingdom and speak of your might, so that all men may know of your mighty acts (PS. 145:11–12).

# 54. The Privileges of the Kingdom

'Therefore, since we are receiving a kingdom that cannot be shaken, let us be thankful, and so worship God acceptably with reverence and awe' (HEB. 12:28).

Father, thank you for giving me your kingdom.

**READING:** MARK 4:26–9
He also said, 'This is what the kingdom of God is like. A man scatters seed on the ground. Night and day, whether he sleeps or gets up, the seed sprouts and grows, though he does not know how. All by itself the soil produces corn – first the stalk, then the ear, then the full kernel in the ear. As soon as the grain is ripe, he puts the sickle to it, because the harvest has come.'

---

The kingdom of God, or the kingdom of heaven, has come with Jesus. It is coming still as His reign is established in the lives of more people. It will come in its fullness when Jesus returns in glory.

The kingdom of heaven is within you as a believer and among men because we believe. The seed of the kingdom will continue to grow in you: first the blade then the ear, then the full corn in the ear.

God wants to see you enjoying the privileges of His kingdom. The kingdom reflects the nature of the king. God is love, so His is a kingdom of love. He is almighty; His is a kingdom of power. He is supernatural; so His kingdom is supernatural. He is righteous; His is a kingdom of righteousness – and so on. The kingdom reflects the nature of the king who rules over it.

There are two spiritual kingdoms, not one. The dominion of darkness reflects the nature of the one who rules over it. Satan does not act according to principles such as those which govern God's kingdom. No, he is unprincipled, a thief who steals, kills and destroys; the deceiver and father of lies, the accuser of the brethren.

But he is no match for God. His dominion is obviously present in the world around us. Many, whether they realise it or not, have submitted their lives to His rule, rather than to the reign of God. Yet when light meets darkness the light prevails. So when we have turned to Christ, Paul explains that God 'has rescued us from the dominion of darkness and brought us into the kingdom of the Son he loves' (Col. 1:13).

You do not belong to the darkness, but to the light. 'For the kingdom of God is not a matter of talk but of power' (1 Cor. 4:20). You have the power of God's positive kingdom which is far greater than the power of Satan's negative kingdom. You have the power to love rather than hate; to forgive rather than be resentful; to give rather than steal; to encourage rather than be jealous – and so on.

Desire that these positive attitudes of the king and His kingdom are demonstrated more and more fully in your life. You can frequently ask yourself; 'Is what I am saying or doing positive or negative? Does it express the life of Jesus and His kingdom?'

You will learn to reign over your circumstances, instead of allowing your circumstances to rule over you. '. . . those who receive God's abundant provision of grace and the gift of righteousness reign in life through the one man, Jesus Christ' (Rom. 5:17). You are to reign in life because you live in the king. You can express His life, His power and His authority. Your life is no longer ruled by the unprincipled prince of darkness, but by the principles of God's kingdom of light. His kingdom is unshakeable.

As you hear and receive the words of Jesus, know that to be

given the kingdom is to have all the riches and resources of this kingdom. It is a kingdom of power, the power that will enable you to reign in life.

**Meditation:**
YOUR FATHER HAS BEEN PLEASED TO GIVE YOU THE KINGDOM (LUKE 12:32).

For the kingdom of God is not a matter of talk but of power (1 COR. 4:20).

For the kingdom of God is . . . righteousness, peace and joy in the Holy Spirit (ROM. 14:17).

**Praise:**
Say to God, 'How awesome are your deeds! So great is your power that your enemies cringe before you' (PS. 66:3).

# 55. The Power of the Kingdom

'I tell you the truth, whatever you bind on earth will be bound in heaven, and whatever you loose on earth will be loosed in heaven' (MATT. 18:18).

Holy Spirit, please enable me to live in the power of the kingdom.

**READING:** MATTHEW 10:7-8
As you go, preach this message: 'The kingdom of heaven is near.' Heal the sick, raise the dead, cleanse those who have leprosy, drive out demons. Freely you have received, freely give.

The privileges of being part of God's kingdom are yours; He has blessed you in Christ with every spiritual blessing in heavenly places. You are a co-heir with Christ of all the Father has to give.

Jesus sent the disciples out with the message of the kingdom, but also to express its power. In His own ministry His words were verified by His works. The same was to be true of His followers. Freely they had received the gift of the kingdom: now they were to give freely of its life and power.

When He sent out the larger number of disciples His instructions were similar: 'When you enter a town and are welcomed, eat what is set before you. Heal the sick who are there and tell them, "The kingdom of God is near you"' (Luke 10:8–9). When they returned they were overjoyed that even the demons had submitted to the authority they had in Jesus's name. Jesus used the opportunity to teach them an important lesson: 'I saw Satan fall like lightning from heaven. I have given you authority to trample on snakes and scorpions and to overcome all the power of the enemy; nothing will harm you. However, do not rejoice that the spirits submit to you, but rejoice that your names are written in heaven' (Luke 10:18–20).

Their names were written in heaven; they belonged to God's kingdom. Satan had been thrown out of heaven when he rebelled against the Lord. So, of course, they had victory over the powers of darkness, and sickness and death. It was not the victory that should be the cause of their joy, but why they had the victory. They belonged to the kingdom of heaven; they possessed the power and authority of God's kingdom.

This is true of you also. Jesus wants to see you exercise the authority you possess as a child of His kingdom. 'I tell you the truth, whatever you bind on earth will be bound in heaven, and whatever you loose on earth will be loosed in heaven' (Matt. 18:18).

You have the authority to act in the name of Jesus, heal in His name, pray in His name. You do not have a gospel of words only, but of power. As you follow the leading of the Holy Spirit, He enables you to exercise this power and authority.

God does not want to see His Church weak, infiltrated by unbelief and the powers of darkness. His children are to be light, a city set on a hill that cannot be hidden. The world is to see and understand that we have the power and authority to bring the victory of Jesus into our personal circumstances and in the situations around us; to reign, not be overcome by events.

The ability to reign begins within you, in the heart attitudes you adopt to your circumstances. You are not the worthless, powerless, weak, spiritual failure you would be without Christ. You live in Him and He in you. Begin to reign over your own circumstances, speaking positively of yourself and of what God will do through you. See each situation as Jesus Himself would view it. Adopt the attitude He would have because you live in Him. The Holy Spirit will help you to do this.

> What would Jesus think?
> What would His attitude be?
> What would He say?
> What would He pray?
> What would He do?

You are in Him. You have the privilege of acting in His name, speaking in His name, praying in His name. As you ask yourself such questions you will be surprised how often the answers will be clear. If this is how Jesus would think, pray, believe and act, then this is what you are to do in this situation. You have the power to do so, but sometimes you may realise you lack the faith to step out in obedience. If this is the case, confess your unbelief to the Lord and He will forgive you. And then spend time 'receiving' His Word, which will inspire faith within you.

---

**Meditation:**
FOR THE KINGDOM OF GOD IS NOT A MATTER OF TALK BUT OF POWER (1 COR. 4:20).

Rejoice that your names are written in heaven (LUKE 10:20).

As you go, preach this message: 'The kingdom of heaven is near' (MATT. 10:7).

**Praise:**
O my Strength, I sing praise to you; you, O God, are my fortress, my loving God (PS. 59:17).

# 56. *Give and Receive*

'But just as you excel in everything – in faith, in speech, in knowledge, in complete earnestness and in your love for us – see that you also excel in this grace of giving' (2 COR. 8:7).

Father, I want to be generous to others; just as you are so generous to me.

**READING:** 2 CORINTHIANS 9:6–9
Remember this: whoever sows sparingly will also reap sparingly, and whoever sows generously will also reap generously. Each man should give what he has decided in his heart to give, not reluctantly or under compulsion, for God loves a cheerful giver. And God is able to make all grace abound to you, so that in all things at all times, having all that you need, you will abound in every good work. As it is written: 'He has scattered abroad his gifts to the poor; his righteousness endures forever.'

Any gardener knows that, no matter how well the soil is prepared, there will be no harvest unless he first plants the seed. If he puts a small amount of seed into the soil he can expect only a small harvest. If he sows generously he will reap generously.

It is a matter of quality as well as of quantity; the wise farmer sows plenty of the finest seed so that he gets a bountiful harvest of the richest quality.

God has chosen to work by the principle of giving in order to receive. He wanted a rich harvest of souls for His kingdom so He sowed the very best seed: He sent His only Son, the Word made flesh. 'I tell you the truth, unless an ear of wheat falls to the ground and dies, it remains only a single seed. But if it dies, it produces many seeds' (John 12:24). If this is the kingdom principle by which God works, we must learn to work along with Him, instead of insisting on receiving first.

It is by the measure you give that you are able to receive the abundance of life He has for you. When you first came to the cross and gave yourself to Jesus, you experienced His life being given to you. He waited until you were prepared to give yourself to Him before He gave Himself to you. This is the principle of God's kingdom at work: 'Give, and it will be given to you. A good measure, pressed down, shaken together and running over, will be poured into your lap. For with the measure you use, it will be measured to you' (Luke 6:38).

Some do not receive answers to prayer because of their lack of giving to God and to others. They are not in a fit spiritual state to be able to do so if they are not 'givers'. Paul gives His teaching on sowing and reaping when speaking of money. There is no doubt that God expects us to be faithful in our financial giving. If we are, we shall receive His abundant measure in return. The world says, 'If you give you will have less.' Jesus says the opposite: 'If you give you will have more.'

This principle relates not only to money, but also to the giving of their lives in every way. To love is to give. John tells us that if we imagine we love God but are not giving to our brothers in need, we are deceiving ourselves. God desires us to be using every opportunity to be giving to Him by giving to one another.

In particular He wants us to be giving into the work of the

kingdom that His purposes may be fulfilled, that His kingdom will come and His will be done on earth as in heaven.

When you plant seed expect a harvest, expect God's abundant measure back to meet your need. When you plant your seed of prayer with faith, water it with praise and continue to thank God until you see the harvest. Jesus taught His disciples to *believe* the harvest as they prayed, rather than waiting for the evidence before they believed.

We know that our God has so much to give; by His grace we have as much to receive. I have hardly begun to receive all that God has to give. What is already mine is still waiting to be appropriated by faith. As I live, not to receive but to give to God, He pours into my life a rich abundance. You will find this is true for you because it is the Word of God. The measure you give will be the measure you get back, but with God it is 'good measure, pressed down, shaken together and running over' (Luke 6:38).

Seek to live by the principles of God's kingdom. These are the principles Jesus lived by and they work!

---

**Meditation:**
GIVE, AND IT WILL BE GIVEN TO YOU (LUKE 6:38).

Whoever sows generously will also reap generously (2 COR. 9:6).

See that you also excel in this grace of giving (2 COR. 8:7).


**Praise:**
Praise be to God, who has not rejected my prayer or withheld his love from me! (PS. 66:20).

# 57. The Measure you Give

'Blessed are the merciful, for they will be shown mercy' (MATT. 5:7).

Father, I want to give to you and to others in the ways that will please you.

---

**READING:** LUKE 6:37–8
Do not judge, and you will not be judged. Do not condemn, and you will not be condemned. Forgive, and you will be forgiven. Give, and it will be given to you. A good measure, pressed down, shaken together and running over, will be poured into your lap. For with the measure you use, it will be measured to you.

---

Because the principle of giving and receiving is a basic principle of God's kingdom, it applies to many areas of Jesus's teaching. 'For with the measure you use, it will be measured to you.' In other words you receive according to the way you give.

This is true of attitudes towards others: 'Do not judge, and you will not be judged.' The inference is clear that if you do judge others you will yourself be judged in the same way. The same is true of condemnation. 'Do not condemn, and you will not be condemned.'

It makes no sense for Jesus to die on the cross to save us from judgment and condemnation, only for us to place ourselves back under judgment and condemnation because of the way in which we treat others!

'Forgive, and you will be forgiven.' The principle works with the positive as well as the negative. But Jesus warns: 'But if you do not forgive me their sins, your Father will not forgive your sins' (Matt. 6:15).

The Lord wants us to express love to others. To receive

love, you need to give love. Some people wait to receive love from others, and are often bitter and accusing that they receive so little. They need to understand the truth that it is in giving they receive. 'Give, and it will be given to you. A good measure, pressed down, shaken together and running over, will be poured into your lap . . .' (Luke 6:38). This is true of love as of everything else.

You gave your life to Him, He gave His life for you. That is a pretty good deal! But you needed to give first. The same is true about receiving the Holy Spirit, healing or any particular anointing or need from God. We give first, surrendering ourselves to Him and then He gives to us.

If you are ever short on receiving from God, consider what you are giving to Him. Let the words of Jesus sink deep into your heart. Give love, forgiveness, mercy; give generously of yourself to Him and to others and expect the good measure in return. 'Blessed are the merciful, for they will be shown mercy' (Matt. 5:7).

If you need to receive from others, stop and consider what you are giving to others. 'It is more blessed to give than to receive' (Acts 20:35). That means you will actually be blessed more in the giving than seeking only to receive!

---

**Meditation:**
FOR WITH THE MEASURE YOU USE, IT WILL BE MEASURED TO YOU (LUKE 6:38).

It is more blessed to give than to receive (ACTS 20:35).

For where your treasure is, there your heart will be also (MATT. 6:21).

**Praise:**
Righteousness and justice are the foundation of your throne; love and faithfulness go before you (PS. 89:14).

# 58. The Command to Love

'How great is the love the Father has lavished on us, that we should be called children of God!' (1 JOHN 3:1).

Holy Spirit, fill me with your love.

### READING: JOHN 15:9–14
As the Father has loved me, so have I loved you. Now remain in my love. If you obey my commands, you will remain in my love, just as I have obeyed my Father's commands and remain in his love. I have told you this so that my joy may be in you and that your joy may be complete. My command is this: Love each other as I have loved you. Greater love has no-one than this, that he lay down his life for his friends. You are my friends if you do what I command.

---

God has expressed His love for us in Jesus – supremely in the cross, but also throughout His ministry.

The Father's love for Jesus was perfect. Whenever Jesus spoke, the Father spoke and acted through Him. He was so concerned to maintain the unity in relationship that if He could not find time to pray in the day because of the pressing demands upon Him from the crowd, then He drew aside quietly at night to be with His Father.

'The Father and I are one,' says everything about their unity, a relationship based on love. The Father was faithful to His Son, leading and guiding Him throughout His earthly ministry, taking Him to the cross, where in love He could pour out His life for us. In love and triumph the Father raised Jesus from the dead.

And Jesus makes this incredible statement. 'As the Father has loved me, so have I loved you.' The Father's love for the Son was perfect and was expressed in practical power throughout His life and ministry. This means that Jesus's love for you is perfect and He desires to express that in practical ways. He will be faithful to you; He will lead you and guide you by His Spirit; He will carry you through traumas and difficulties bringing you to victory.

Jesus says; 'Now remain in my love.' The tense in Greek is continuous: 'Go on continually living in my love, remaining and resting in my love.'

You need never ask Jesus to love you; He already does. You need never question His love for He will not withdraw His love from you. His love is a fact, the greatest fact upon which to build your life.

The way to remain in the knowledge and power of Jesus's love is to obey His words. Love is not sentiment, but is expressed in a true desire to do God's will in your life.

Because He is love, His command to us is to love. 'And this is His command: to believe in the name of his Son, Jesus Christ, and to love one another as he commanded us' (1 John 3:23). He loves us as the Father has loved Him; and so Jesus tells us to love one another in the same way He loves us. This means laying down our lives for one another, even as He laid His life down for us, being faithful to one another, reliable and dependable; encouraging one another; forgiving, merciful and gracious; ready to serve humbly.

The more you know of God's love for you, the more love you will share with others. John points out; 'Dear friends, since God so loved us, we also ought to love one another. No-one has ever seen God; but if we love each other, God lives in us and his love is made complete in us' (1 John 4:11–12).

Hear Jesus speaking to you now, assuring you that He loves you in the same way that the Father loved Him. His love for you is both perfect and practical. All His divine power is behind this love, the love in which He tells you to abide.

---

**Meditation:**
AS THE FATHER HAS LOVED ME, SO HAVE I LOVED YOU. NOW REMAIN IN MY LOVE (JOHN 15:9).

If you obey my commands, you will remain in my love (JOHN 15:10).

Love each other as I have loved you (JOHN 15:12).

**Praise:**
Give thanks to the Lord of lords: his love endures for ever (PS. 136:3).

# 59. Love one Another

'Whoever loves his brother lives in the light, and there is nothing in him to make him stumble' (1 JOHN 2:10).

Lord Jesus, please help me to love others as you have loved me.

### READING: 1 JOHN 4:7–12
Dear friends, let us love one another, for love comes from God. Everyone who loves has been born of God and knows God. Whoever does not love does not know God, because God is love. This is how God showed his love among us: He sent his one and only Son into the world that we might live through him. This is love: not that we loved God, but that he loved us and sent his Son as an atoning sacrifice for our sins.
　　Dear friends, since God so loved us, we also ought to love one another.

When Jesus gave this command to love one another as He has loved us, He explained this would mean laying down our lives for our friends. What does this involve? Living not for your own ends, but to love and serve others. By doing this, you love and serve the Lord.

The message of John's first epistle is challenging and uncompromising; you can assess your true relationship with God by the way in which you relate to fellow Christians. The one is a reflection of the other. You cannot truly love God, unless you love your brother also. Listen to what the Holy Spirit says through John: 'This is the message you heard from the beginning: We should love one another' (1 John 3:11). 'This is how we know what love is: Jesus Christ laid down his life for us. And we ought to lay down our lives for our brothers' (1 John 3:16).

He explains what this involves in practice:

> If anyone has material possessions and sees his brother in need but has no pity on him, how can the love of God be in him? Dear children, let us not love with words or tongue but with actions and in truth (1 John 3:17–18).
>
> Dear friends, let us love one another, for love comes from God. Everyone who loves has been born of God and knows God (1 John 4:7).
>
> No-one has ever seen God: but if we love each other, God lives in us and his love is made complete in us (1 John 4:12).
>
> We love because he first loved us. If anyone says, 'I love God,' yet hates his brother, he is a liar . . . (1 John 4:19–20).
>
> And he has given us this command: Whoever loves God must also love his brother (1 John 4:21).
>
> This is how we know that we love the children of God: by loving God and carrying out his commands (1 John 5:2).

These verses speak for themselves. There is no such thing as a costless Christianity. It cost Jesus His life to love us, and it costs us our lives to express His love to others. Wherever you go as a Christian you are a witness of His love and you have practical opportunities to express that love. How much you will do so depends on the extent to which you have died to yourself in order that you might live for Jesus.

He never expects you to love without making the resources of His love available to you. And so John also reminds his readers, 'But you have an anointing from the Holy One' (1 John 2:20). '. . . the anointing you received from him remains in you' (1 John 2:27). 'And so we know and rely on the love God has for us' (1 John 4:16).

Receive His love afresh as you receive His words. And rejoice that you are one through whom He has chosen to express His love to others.

Understand that your life can be a great blessing to the Lord and to others as you express His love He has put within by the Holy Spirit.

---

**Meditation:**
AS I HAVE LOVED YOU, SO YOU MUST LOVE ONE ANOTHER (JOHN 13:34).

Dear friends, let us love one another, for love comes from God (1 JOHN 4:7).

If we love each other, God lives in us and his love is made complete in us (1 JOHN 4:12).

**Praise:**
How priceless is your unfailing love! (PS. 36:7).

# 60. The Spirit's Love

'Dear children, let us not love with words or tongue but with actions and in truth' (1 JOHN 3:18).

Father, I want to express your love in my life.

**READING:** 1 CORINTHIANS 13:4–8
Love is patient, love is kind. It does not envy, it does not boast, it is not proud. It is not rude, it is not self-seeking, it is not easily angered, it keeps no record of wrongs. Love does not delight in evil but rejoices with the truth. It always protects, always trusts, always hopes, always perseveres.
Love never fails.

---

Paul speaks here of the qualities of God's love, the love the Holy Spirit puts within our hearts. Naturally we can be very impatient, unkind, envious, boasting, proud, rude, self-seeking, angry and unforgiving. These are the expressions of the flesh opposed to the Spirit. To each individual some of these will be greater problems than others. But all of us would have to acknowledge our guilt in the wrong attitudes and reactions we have towards some people at certain times.

However, the Holy Spirit creates within us the attitudes and reactions of Jesus. You cannot imagine any of these fleshly expressions in His life. The amazing thing about the Spirit's activity within us is that He changes us so that we can express more of Jesus in our relationships.

Unfortunately, the Holy Spirit does not produce instant perfection in our lives. If you examine your relationships, even briefly, you will see that you express many of the positive aspects of love mentioned by Paul – towards certain people! However, there may be others of whom you are less tolerant and to whom it seems very difficult to express God's love.

These are the relationships with which He wants to help if you will allow Him. As you confess the unloving things, so then you can ask the Spirit to produce in you the positive aspects of Jesus's love.

He wants to teach us to love others for their sake, and not out of selfish motives. Jesus reminds us that even unbelievers love those who will love them in return. The Christian is called to love, even if his love is taken for granted, or even rejected.

Often our unwillingness to love others comes out of our own insecurity. For some reason we are afraid to love or allow others to love us. Ultimately this is an indication of a person's lack of assurance in God's love for him. You can love if you are confident in God's love for you, even if that love is rebuffed. Perhaps you rejected love shown you by other Christians before you came to know Him, because you felt challenged in some way or convicted about your need of God. Similarly your love is likely to be rejected on occasions. Do not allow this to deter you from loving others. Try to understand what is going on in the other person and make allowances for any insecurities they may be experiencing.

A lack of love can be the result of a lack of brokenness in the believer. He has not truly submitted himself to the Lord. He wants to remain in the driving seat in his life and is ruled in many ways by pride and selfishness. He is likely to love only when it suits him, when it is not too demanding or inconvenient to do so.

We can rejoice in the provision God has made for us by filling us with His Spirit of love. The one who is filled has to use that love, expressing it to others. His willingness to do this will depend on His willingness to co-operate with God in His purposes.

Fresh resources of His love are always available for He never comes to the end of His giving to us. As you feed on God's Word know that He is speaking love and communicating that love to you.

**Meditation:**
THE SPIRIT WILL TAKE FROM WHAT IS
MINE AND MAKE IT KNOWN TO YOU
(JOHN 16:15).

The anointing you received from him remains in you
(1 JOHN 2:27).

We love because he first loved us (1 JOHN 4:19).

**Praise:**
Give thanks to the Lord, for he is good. His love
endures for ever (PS. 136:1).

# 61. *His Witnesses*

'Listen, my dear brothers: Has not God chosen those who are
poor in the eyes of the world to be rich in faith and to inherit
the kingdom he promised those who love him?' (JAS. 2:5).

Father, I want to bear much fruit for your glory.

**READING:** JAMES 2:14–22
What good is it, my brothers, if a man claims to have
faith but has no deeds? Can such faith save him?
Suppose a brother or sister is without clothes and
daily food. If one of you says to him, 'Go, I wish you
well; keep warm and well fed,' but does nothing about
his physical needs, what good is it? In the same way,
faith by itself, if it is not accompanied by action, is
dead.

But someone will say, 'You have faith; I have
deeds.'

Show me your faith without deeds, and I will show
you my faith by what I do. You believe that there is

one God. Good! Even the demons believe that – and shudder.

You foolish man, do you want evidence that faith without deeds is useless? Was not our ancestor Abraham considered righteous for what he did when he offered his son Isaac on the altar? You see that his faith and his actions were working together, and his faith was made complete by what he did.

---

Faith will result in positive action. Faith comes through hearing God's Word, believing what He says *and acting upon it*.

Love is not true love unless it results in positive action, laying down our lives for our friends – living for them rather than for ourselves, rejoicing in the opportunities we have to give and to serve.

The enemy wants you to be passive. He does not mind very much if people indulge in super-spiritual talk so long as they do not produce any fruit. Jesus said, 'This is to my Father's glory, that you bear much fruit, showing yourselves to be my disciples' (John 15:8).

God wants you to be active, not passive. This does not mean that you are to go around in a blaze of self-effort; rather you are to follow the leading of the Spirit who will lead you into what the Father wants you to be doing actively, at the same time empowering you to do it.

To James, faith without works is dead. In other words, it is not true faith unless it results in positive action. Some try to put an unreal division between what James and Paul say about faith. The faith that justifies, which makes us acceptable to God and leads to new birth, will result in fruitfulness. When God speaks He expects obedience, which always leads to fruitfulness. He leads His children into activity, not passivity.

James says something else of great importance here. Believing there is a God is not sufficient to please Him, or to bring salvation into a person's life. Even demons believe there is only one God, but that does not make them Christian! They are utterly opposed to all things Christian.

Your faith is not a series of verbal statements outlining what you believe about God, but the putting of your trust in Him in everyday practical situations, believing He will manifest His love and power through you; His supernatural life shining through your natural life. So, James says, faith and action go together.

The fields are ripe for the harvest. God is able to use you to bring the gospel of His kingdom to others in practical ways; through the way you love others by serving them; through your faith bringing God's supernatural power into daily events; through your witness in word and deed.

What does God want you to do specifically? He will show you if you want to know. But you can begin where you are by loving and serving those around you, by expecting His supernatural power to change circumstances, by telling others the good news that God wants to give them a kingdom.

Hear Jesus encouraging you to fruitfulness. He wants to see His Father glorified in your life by what the Holy Spirit does through you. Remember, Paul says that the only thing that counts is faith being expressed in love.

---

**Meditation:**
THIS IS TO MY FATHER'S GLORY, THAT YOU BEAR MUCH FRUIT, SHOWING YOURSELVES TO BE MY DISCIPLES (JOHN 15:8).

If a man remains in me and I in him, he will bear much fruit; apart from me you can do nothing (JOHN 15:5).

The only thing that counts is faith expressing itself through love (GAL. 5:6).

**Praise:**
I am still confident of this: I will see the goodness of the Lord in the land of the living (PS. 27:13).

# 62. *Unity*

'If I give all I possess to the poor and surrender my body to the flames, but have not love, I gain nothing' (1 COR. 13:3).

Holy Spirit, help me to know my unity with all who are in Christ.

### READING: EPHESIANS 4:1–6
I urge you to live a life worthy of the calling you have received. Be completely humble and gentle; be patient, bearing with one another in love. Make every effort to keep the unity of the Spirit through the bond of peace. There is one body and one Spirit – just as you were called to one hope when you were called – one Lord, one faith, one baptism; one God and Father of all, who is over all and through all and in all.

---

The Holy Spirit is able to produce a unity of love that transcends any differences between Christians. To the world there appears to be many churches, but in fact there is only one Church, the Church of the Lord Jesus Christ. All who are born again of the Spirit are part of that one Church, regardless of their denominational affiliation. Jesus Christ Himself is the head of that one Church.

He desires to see unity in His body, which is the way Paul describes the Church. Jesus prayed for this unity before going to the cross. 'May they be brought to complete unity to let the world know that you sent me and have loved them even as you have loved me' (John 17:23). This unity is to be a witness of God's love to the world. Jesus is speaking about unity in the relationship between Christians, even among those who are part of the same expression of local fellowship.

Jesus reveals Himself to Christians 'in order that the love you have for me may be in them and that I myself may be in them' (John 17:26). This is an amazing prayer, that the

Father's own love for the Son might be in us; and that Jesus Himself might live in us.

When we love, we allow the presence of Jesus to shine through our lives as light in the midst of darkness. How important, then, not to allow differences to divide us, to have a proper respect for other born-again believers, whether you agree on all points of doctrine or not. The Spirit of truth will guide us into all the truth, says Jesus. That is not the starting-point but where the Spirit will lead us.

How important to honour one another, encourage each other and speak well of one another. We are not involved in competition with other believers, but are seeking to express the love and faith of Jesus to an unbelieving world. So Paul says: 'Be devoted to one another in brotherly love. Honour one another above yourselves' (Rom. 12:10).

We can further the disunity of the Church by the negative attitudes we have and the negative things we say, even about others in our own fellowship. Or we can increase the unity among Christians by concentrating on the love and faith which unite us, using every opportunity to work with others to see God's kingdom on earth.

Unfortunately, Christians often concentrate on what divides them instead of finding their true unity in the love of Christ. Openness to the influence of God's Spirit will draw believers into a new sense of unity not necessarily of ecclesiastical order, but of love and faith.

Confess the unity you have with others and express that in the love the Spirit gives you. Use opportunities that arise to understand and listen to what other Christians can teach you of your common life in Christ. Stand against any unbelief or compromise of God's Word – but always with love. You are to love your brother in Christ, even if you don't agree with everything he says!

---

**Meditation:**
BE PATIENT, BEARING WITH ONE ANOTHER IN LOVE (EPH. 4:2).

I pray . . . that all of them may be one, Father, just as you are in me and I am in you (JOHN 17:20–1).

Make every effort to keep the unity of the Spirit through the bond of peace (EPH. 4:3).

**Praise:**
How good and pleasant it is when brothers live together in unity! . . . For there the Lord bestows his blessing (PS. 133:1, 3).

# 63. Spread the Kingdom

'The creation waits in eager expectation for the sons of God to be revealed' (ROM. 8:19).

Father, please use me to show others the way into your kingdom.

### READING: PHILIPPIANS 2:14–16
Do everything without complaining or arguing, so that you may become blameless and pure, children of God without fault in a crooked and depraved generation, in which you shine like stars in the universe as you hold out the word of life – in order that I may boast on the day of Christ that I did not run or labour for nothing.

---

The world is full of people in great need physically, socially and economically. Yet their greatest need is to be made alive spiritually, and this can only happen through a personal relationship with Jesus. The Christian is not to try to make himself acceptable to others by adopting the standards and ideals of the world. He wants to bring his thoughts, speech and actions into line with God's will, to live as a child of God's kingdom, demonstrating to others the benefits of belonging to His kingdom.

'The creation waits in eager expectation for the sons of God to be revealed' (Rom. 8:19). You are one of these sons. The world needs to hear the Word of God, not the ideas and opinions of men. They will pass away with them, but God's words are eternal truth. When God's children speak His Word under the authority of the Holy Spirit the truth can penetrate to the heart and evoke a definite response. But that Word needs to live in the one who speaks it; then he will be able to speak heart to heart, rather than mind to mind.

The initial response can sometimes appear negative because the truth can seem uncomfortable. It is better for someone to feel uncomfortable if this will lead him or her to repentance and new life! Paul said: 'You know that I have not hesitated to preach anything that would be helpful to you' (Acts 20:20). Paul appreciated that there was bound to be friction where the kingdom of light confronts the kingdom of darkness, the kingdom of this world.

God's Word will work for anyone who believes because it is truth. A fundamental truth such as 'God loves you' needs to be supplemented with an understanding of the nature of His grace, mercy and forgiveness. People need to know He is the God of promise, who is faithful to His Word, and they need to be shown how they can receive the gift of His kingdom from Him. He wants to meet with them in their daily situations in His supernatural power, to exercise His reign over them that they also may 'reign in life'.

You can help these things to live for others if they are real for you. The rich inheritance you have in Christ will become more real as you share your faith with others. 'I pray that you may be active in sharing your faith, so that you will have full understanding of every good thing we have in Christ' (Philem. v.6). Take this truth to heart!

Do not allow fear and self-consciousness to prevent you from speaking out what needs to be said. And don't allow your conversation to be reduced to the negative level of the world around you, where others complain and argue without faith, where there is much bitterness, resentment, jealousy and anger. Speak as a child of God's kingdom, the kingdom of righteousness, joy and peace in the Holy Spirit. Spread these qualities by the things you say and do.

If the Word is spoken in the power of the Spirit, things will happen to people because 'the word of God is living and active. Sharper than any double-edged sword, it penetrates even to dividing soul and spirit' (Heb. 4:12). It cuts straight to the heart of the listener. Sinners are brought under conviction, saints are encouraged and God confirms His Word with demonstrations of power.

This was how Jesus and the early Church communicated the gospel. This is the method needed in this generation. We need to speak the truth to the world in the power of the Holy Spirit and see that Word confirmed with signs and wonders.

---

**Meditation:**
FREELY YOU HAVE RECEIVED, FREELY GIVE (MATT. 10:8).

Whoever acknowledges me before men, I will also acknowledge him before my Father in heaven (MATT. 10:32).

What I tell you in the dark, speak in the daylight (MATT. 10:27).

**Praise:**
Declare his glory among the nations, his marvellous deeds among all peoples (PS. 96:3).

# PART SEVEN

# YOUR LIFE OF DISCIPLESHIP

# 64. Following Christ

Anyone who does not take his cross and follow me is not worthy of me (MATT. 10:38).

I want to follow you, Jesus.

**READING:** LUKE 9:23-6
Then he said to them all: 'If anyone would come after me, he must deny himself and take up his cross daily and follow me. For whoever wants to save his life will lose it, but whoever loses his life for me will save it. What good is it for a man to gain the whole world, and yet lose or forfeit his very self? If anyone is ashamed of me and my words, the Son of Man will be ashamed of him when he comes in his glory and in the glory of the Father and of the holy angels.'

As soon as Jesus began to speak about His rejection and crucifixion, He also spoke about a cross the disciples would have to carry. This cross was not only for the original twelve, but for anyone who wanted to follow Jesus.

The cross all disciples have to carry is different from that which Jesus Himself suffered. The crucifixion of God's Son was a unique event, never to be repeated. He carried the sin of all humanity, our pain and sickness, grief and sorrow. On the cross He overcame the devil and all his works.

There is nothing that has to be, or could ever be, added to the victory of the cross. God's intention is that we learn to live in the power of this victory He has gained for us.

We must be careful, therefore, that we do not carry the wrong cross. Sometimes Christians talk about being punished for their sins and suggest that is the cross they must carry. This is not right. Jesus bore our punishment on the cross so that we might know God's gracious mercy and forgiveness, and be spared the punishment we rightly deserve.

Sometimes it is suggested that sickness is the cross we have to carry. But Jesus bore our infirmities and sicknesses on the cross and by His stripes we have been healed. The cross was the answer to sickness. If someone imagines that being sick is suffering for the kingdom, they had better examine the Scriptures more carefully.

Jesus makes clear the nature of our cross as Christians or as His disciples. It is the cross of self-denial: 'If anyone would come after me, *he must deny himself* and take up his cross daily and follow me' (Luke 9:23). This involves surrendering ourselves to the Lordship of Jesus. It is not what we want that matters, but what He wants.

He makes it clear that those who follow Him will experience persecution, rejection and ridicule. There will be plenty of cost. But this cross is something we willingly take up every day. We are prepared to face the cost of being faithful witnesses in a world full of negative unbelief and darkness.

We do not enjoy the cost but it is inevitable, if we are to be faithful to the Lord. Jesus experienced such cost throughout His ministry, but with the right attitude; 'who for the joy set before him endured the cross, scorning its shame' (Heb. 12:2). For us the cost can take a variety of forms: making sacrifices of time or money in order to serve others; the cost of a disciplined spiritual life in prayer and meditation; the submission of our wills to God's will, agreeing to do what we do not want to do; the cost of loving others, of bringing the gospel to those who do not know Jesus; persecution and ridicule for professing faith in Him; standing by the principles of the Word, even if this includes financial loss.

And so James tells us: 'Consider it pure joy, my brothers, whenever you face trials of many kinds, because you know that the testing of your faith develops perseverance' (Jas. 1:2–3). Whatever the cost, the rewards are always much greater. And no cost we face could possibly compare with what Jesus suffered for us.

Hear the promise of Jesus's words. Don't concentrate on the cost but on the joy of knowing you are serving Him. Remember that you cannot give to Him without receiving a much greater reward.

**Meditation:**
WHOEVER LOSES HIS LIFE FOR ME WILL
FIND IT (MATT. 16:25).

Come, follow me (MATT. 4:19).

Anyone who does not take his cross and follow me is
not worthy of me (MATT. 10:38).

**Praise:**
How beautiful on the mountains are the feet of those
who bring good news, who proclaim peace, who
bring good tidings, who proclaim salvation, who say
to Zion, 'Your God reigns!' (ISA. 52:7).

# 65. Crucified with Christ

'I have been crucified with Christ and I no longer live, but
Christ lives in me. The life I live in the body, I live by faith in
the Son of God, who loved me and gave himself for me' (GAL.
2:20).

Father, I recognise my life belongs totally to you.

**READING: 1 CORINTHIANS 6:19–20**
Do you not know that your body is a temple of the
Holy Spirit, who is in you, whom you have received
from God? You are not your own; you were bought at
a price. Therefore honour God with your body.

---

Jesus took you, not only your sin to the cross. Through His
blood you can receive forgiveness for your sins. Through the
cross the power of sin can be broken in your life. This is why
Paul said: 'I have been crucified with Christ and I no longer

live, but Christ lives in me. The life I live in the body, I live by faith in the Son of God, who loved me and gave himself for me' (Gal. 2:20). Jesus not only took Saul's sin to the cross: He took Saul of Tarsus so that his old life might be put to death and he be given a new life, a new nature.

This not only shows you the great power of the cross but faces you with another truth. Your life does not belong to you. Everything you are and all that you have belongs to the Lord.

When Jesus went to the cross, God the Father paid the price for you with the blood of His Son, in order that you would belong completely to Him. You have no life, no identity, nothing apart from Him. The Father wanted *you* for His child and *you* in the kingdom, not your sins. He cleansed you to make you a sacred temple of His presence in the world.

The Lord desires more than mental assent to the truth that everything you are and have belongs to Him. The test comes when he wants to take possession of some part of your life, but comes into conflict with your will. We do not always want to be obedient. Even when we know what is right, we do not necessarily want to do it. To live as a child of His kingdom is to recognise the rights God has over us and the claims He can rightly make upon us.

God does not seek to take away from you as you commit your life to Him; He already owns every part of you. This is a revelation that brings great freedom into your life. Whatever you yield to the Lord is His already; to hold something back from Him denies His ownership of your life. His desire is to work in and through you. Paul speaks of 'the glorious riches of this mystery, which is Christ in you, the hope of glory' (Col. 1:27).

Because the old Saul no longer lived, Christ could live in the new man, Paul. The apostle could now live by faith in God's Son and all the riches He had made available.

Consider this: Christ lives in you to express His life and love through you by the power of the Holy Spirit. The person you once were is dead and buried with Christ, as signified in your water baptism. He wants to flow out of your innermost being like rivers of living water. You belong to Him. By co-operating with Him and His purposes for your life, He will have His way and make you a blessing to Him and to others. It is no longer you who lives but Christ in you.

You are set free from the bondage of self. You do not have to strive to accomplish things for God; He will work through you as you recognise who holds the true ownership of your life and submit to His purposes. His commands need not be burdensome; you will delight to do His will.

The Holy God is able to express His holy life through you by His Holy Spirit. All He needs is your co-operation. Consider the privileges of being called and chosen by God. Why you? This is a question you will never answer satisfactorily. You can only be thankful for all His love and grace in choosing you to be His own possession, one in whom He lives.

---

**Meditation:**
YOU ARE NOT YOUR OWN; YOU WERE BOUGHT AT A PRICE. THEREFORE HONOUR GOD WITH YOUR BODY (1 COR. 6:19–20).

Your body is a temple of the Holy Spirit, who is in you (1 COR. 6:19).

The life I live in the body, I live by faith in the Son of God, who loved me and gave himself for me (GAL. 2:20).

**Praise:**
For with you is the fountain of life; in your light we see light (PS. 36:9).

# 66. *Agreeing with God*

'Blessed rather are those who hear the word of God and obey it' (LUKE 11:28).


Lord Jesus, may I never argue with your words.


**READING:** MATTHEW 16:13–23

When Jesus came to the region of Caesarea Philippi, he asked his disciples, 'Who do people say the Son of Man is?' They replied, 'Some say John the Baptist; others say Elijah; and still others, Jeremiah or one of the prophets.'

'But what about you?' he asked. 'Who do you say I am?'

Simon Peter answered. 'You are the Christ, the Son of the living God.'

Jesus replied, 'Blessed are you, Simon son of Jonah, for this was not revealed to you by man, but by my Father in heaven. And I tell you that you are Peter, and on this rock I will build my church, and the gates of Hades will not overcome it. I will give you the keys of the kingdom of heaven; whatever you bind on earth will be bound in heaven, and whatever you loose on earth will be loosed in heaven.' Then he warned his disciples not to tell anyone that he was the Christ.

From that time on Jesus began to explain to his disciples that he must go to Jerusalem and suffer many things at the hands of the elders, chief priests and teachers of the law, and that he must be killed and on the third day be raised to life.

Peter took him aside and began to rebuke him. 'Never, Lord!' he said. 'This shall never happen to you!'

Jesus turned and said to Peter, 'Out of my sight,

Satan! You are a stumbling block to me; you do not
have in mind the things of God, but the things of men.'

---

This is the moment of truth, the time for the disciples to
understand who Jesus is. It is Peter who comes out with the
heaven-inspired declaration: 'You are the Christ, the Son of
the living God.' Jesus commends him and uses this opportunity to tell the disciples they share His authority to bind and
loose. But He also prophesies His forthcoming passion,
crucifixion and resurrection.

This is too much for Peter. He wants to argue. How can
such a thing be true for the Messiah, the Christ, God's Son?
'Never Lord! This shall never happen to you!' (Matt. 16:22) he
says.

Peter has made a serious mistake. One minute he is recognising the divinity of Jesus, acknowledging Him as God's Son:
the next he is daring to argue with Him. Satan is the one who
argues with God's Word. From being the mouthpiece of a
revelation from the Father, Peter has become a spokesman for
the enemy!

What a warning for us all. When we speak against God's
Word, when we want to argue with what He says, we are
siding with His enemy. This is not a clever thing to do! We
argue sometimes because what God says is beyond our understanding; and other times because we do not like what He is
saying.

Peter could not, at this stage, understand why Jesus should
need to go to the cross. Neither did he like what he had heard.
He listened to his emotions rather than to the Lord. He had
grown to love Jesus and could not bear the thought of His
'suffering many things' and being killed.

The lesson we need to learn from this is to submit intellectual understanding, our emotions and wills to God's Word,
every part of our souls being brought into line with what He
says.

This does not mean the Lord wants us to be non-intellectual.
Far from it. Peter's mind needed to be expanded and his

understanding of Old Testament prophecies extended, before he could appreciate the need for the cross. The Spirit of God challenges us to think expansively. The natural mind diminishes God and His abilities.

There are always those who want to raise their reason above the inspiration of Scripture. In effect, their thinking is too small to encompass God's thoughts and understanding. Because of their pride they imagine the Lord must be confined to their own understanding of Him, which is often minute.

Allow the Scriptures to speak to you, enlarging your understanding as well as speaking life and healing to you. Every word is food for you as a disciple of Jesus. When He speaks to you don't argue with Him. Whatever He asks of you, do it. Learn from what He says and believe His promises.

---

**Meditation:**
MAN DOES NOT LIVE ON BREAD ALONE, BUT ON EVERY WORD THAT COMES FROM THE MOUTH OF GOD (MATT. 4:4).

My food . . . is to do the will of him who sent me and to finish his work (JOHN 4:34).

Do whatever he tells you (JOHN 2:5).

**Praise:**
How sweet are your promises to my taste, sweeter than honey to my mouth! (PS. 119:103).

# 67. Serving in His Name

'I have made you known to them, and will continue to make you known in order that the love you have for me may be in them and that I myself may be in them' (JOHN 17:26).

Lord Jesus, help me to serve humbly.

**READING:** MATTHEW 25:34–6
Then the King will say to those on his right, 'Come, you who are blessed by my Father; take your inheritance, the kingdom prepared for you since the creation of the world. For I was hungry and you gave me something to eat, I was thirsty and you gave me something to drink, I was a stranger and you invited me in, I needed clothes and you clothed me, I was sick and you looked after me, I was in prison and you came to visit me.'

---

The greatest in the kingdom shall be the least of all, the one who is willing to serve. This is another kingdom principle. Because Jesus lived the kingdom life perfectly while on earth, He came as the humble servant of all. 'Instead, the greatest among you should be like the youngest, and the one who rules like the one who serves' (Luke 22:26).

What a privilege to be used by the king! What a privilege that He should live in you and work through you. Even when you have done everything He wants, you are still an unworthy servant, says Jesus (Luke 17:10). And yet He gives back to you immeasurably more than you give to others, promising to reward you for all that you do.

It is as we reach out with the life, the love and the power of the king that we fulfil our mission now as children of the kingdom. The love of God is very practical and if this is to be expressed in our lives this will involve being prepared to serve others in whatsoever ways He asks us. We shall not be fruitful by closing our eyes to the needs around us. Love is practical and is expressed in giving and serving others. What you are prepared to give to God is shown by what you give to serve others, the ways in which you use your time, abilities or money.

You can look at yourself and say, 'I don't have enough love', or you can recognise the truth that God has given you the Father's love for the Son. This means you can give, love and act instead of only talking about what needs to be done. 'For the kingdom of God is not a matter of talk but of power' (1 Cor. 4:20). It is not enough to express concern if you have the resources to meet the need. God has given you the power to love, to serve, to work miracles in His name.

Before you aspire to great things in God, remember that Jesus says you are to prove faithful in small things. Many want to achieve spectacular results which will appear impressive, but they don't want to get their hands dirty. They want recognition, but not humbly to serve others.

You do not have to go searching for a ministry. God puts in front of your eyes and under your nose what He wants you to do, and the people He wants you to love. And He never asks you to do anything without making available to you the resources to do it. You do not have to rely upon your natural resources and abilities. When these are submitted to Him and His use, you find His supernatural resources and ability are readily available.

In the above passage, those who had served the Lord faithfully were astonished at the way He commended them. What they had done seemed so natural to them, expressing the love and compassion He had placed in their hearts. By comparison, those who were filled with self-concern were oblivious to the needs around them.

Often you may feel incapable and inadequate to love, serve and meet the needs of others. Be encouraged; the secret is Christ in you. The Holy Spirit will help and enable you. Even now you can receive afresh the resources of God's love; they are always available to you.

**Meditation:**
I AM AMONG YOU AS ONE WHO SERVES
(LUKE 22:27).

Serve wholeheartedly, as if you were serving the Lord
(EPH. 6:7).

Not everyone who says to me, 'Lord, Lord,' will enter
the kingdom of heaven, but only he who does the will
of my Father who is in heaven (MATT. 7:21).

**Praise:**
Your love, O Lord, reaches to the heavens, your
faithfulness to the skies (PS. 36:5).

# 68. *Using Your Authority*

'Or again, how can anyone enter a strong man's house and
carry off his possessions unless he first ties up the strong man?
Then he can rob his house' (MATT. 12:29).

Lord Jesus, I want to exercise the authority you give me.

**READING:** 2 CORINTHIANS 10:3–5
For though we live in the world, we do not wage war
as the world does. The weapons we fight with are not
the weapons of the world. On the contrary, they have
divine power to demolish strongholds. We demolish
arguments and every pretension that sets itself up
against the knowledge of God, and we take captive
every thought to make it obedient to Christ.

Some come to initial faith in Jesus proclaiming, 'You are the Christ', without moving on in obedience to the Lord. God calls us not only to initial faith, but to a lifetime of faith in Him. For faith brings the victory of Jesus into the present circumstances.

Many Christians are ignorant of the spiritual warfare in which they need to be engaged. They do not appreciate the truth of what Paul teaches: 'For our struggle is not against flesh and blood, but against the rulers, against the authorities, against the powers of this dark world and against the spiritual forces of evil in the heavenly realms' (Eph. 6:12).

Christians need to take authority over spiritual forces which seek to rule over nations, places and individuals; to bind the oppressive powers of Satan which want to hinder them in their walk of faith and obedience. They need to pray for people, but also against the powers of darkness which oppose them.

Some do not recognise the powers behind the difficulties they experience. They pray about a situation without binding these powers and commanding them to release the situation. Some do not receive the victory in their sickness because they fail to exercise their authority as children of the kingdom, praying against the powers of darkness which perpetrate sickness. There were several occasions when Jesus commanded healing by releasing people from bondage to evil powers.

Satan wants to capitalise on any area of weakness in your life and to try and put you into oppressive bondage. When this happens you need repentance for the sin, but you also need to exercise authority over the enemy, standing firm against him and commanding him to go. In this way you will be loosed from the oppression and you can then ask the Holy Spirit to strengthen you. You will be amazed at the victory which comes into your life when you do this.

You do not gain the victory by raking around in the past, or looking in upon yourself, but by proclaiming the power of the blood of Jesus which frees you from the past and from every form of oppressive evil. Do not be afraid to dismiss the powers of darkness with the authority you have as God's child. Command them to depart, to stop oppressing you. When confronting the powers of darkness it is worth remembering that if you expect a battle you will have a battle; if you anticipate victory you will have victory. 'I proclaim the victory of Jesus over Satan and all his works. Depart from me all you powers of darkness, you have no claim upon my life.' When you deal with the enemy be firm as you would be with a naughty child. You are telling him what to do.

There may be times when you will sense you are engaged in a spiritual battle as you pray in the Holy Spirit. Continue to 'pray through' until you are assured you have the victory. This is the phrase many of the great men of prayer have used. Persevere; do not give up, even if you experience on occasions that you have not established the victory completely in one session. Remember, the spiritual forces of heaven are infinitely greater than those of the evil one.

First you need to hear the Lord giving personal revelation of your authority as a child of His kingdom.

---

**Meditation:**
SUBMIT YOURSELVES, THEN, TO GOD. RESIST THE DEVIL, AND HE WILL FLEE FROM YOU (JAS. 4:7).

He drove out the spirits with a word and healed all the sick (MATT. 8:16).

Encourage and rebuke with all authority (TITUS 2:15).

**Praise:**
The Lord reigns for ever; he has established his throne for judgment (PS. 9:7).

# 69. The Name of Jesus

'And everyone who calls on the name of the Lord will be saved' (ACTS 2:21).

Father, I want to use the name of Jesus with power and authority.

**READING:** ACTS 3:1–10, 16
One day Peter and John were going up to the temple at the time of prayer – at three in the afternoon. Now a man crippled from birth was being carried to the temple gate called Beautiful, where he was put every day to beg from those going into the temple courts. When he saw Peter and John about to enter, he asked them for money. Peter looked straight at him, as did John. Then Peter said, 'Look at us!' So the man gave them his attention, expecting to get something from them.

Then Peter said, 'Silver or gold I do not have, but what I have I give you. In the name of Jesus Christ of Nazareth, walk.' Taking him by the right hand, he helped him up, and instantly the man's feet and ankles became strong. He jumped to his feet and began to walk. Then he went with them into the temple courts, walking and jumping, and praising God. When all the people saw him walking and praising God, they recognised him as the same man who used to sit begging at the temple gate called Beautiful, and they were filled with wonder and amazement at what had happened to him . . . By faith in the name of Jesus, this man whom you see and know was made strong. It is Jesus' name and the faith that comes through him that has given this complete healing to him, as you can all see.

The name of Jesus is above every other name and means 'Saviour' or 'the Lord saves'. Jesus saves from sin and death, from condemnation and darkness, from the devil and the powers of hell, from sickness and grief. He saves us for Himself, choosing a people who will live for Him, extending His kingdom on earth; a people who will be holy and blameless in His sight.

Because His name is above every other name, at the name of Jesus every knee shall bow 'in heaven and on earth and under the earth, and every tongue confess that Jesus Christ is Lord, to the glory of God the Father' (PHIL. 2:10–11). All will ultimately have to acknowledge the authority of Jesus and the power of His name. 'Salvation is found in no-one else, for there is no other name under heaven given to men by which we must be saved' (Acts 4:12).

Salvation means healing. The name of Jesus stands for the total salvation of spirit, soul and body made possible through the life, death and resurrection of God's Son. When He gives His commission to the Church, Jesus says that believers will drive out demons in His name and 'they will place their hands on sick people, and they will get well' (Mark 16:18).

We see these words being fulfilled by Peter and John as they heal the crippled beggar. When they had to explain to the people why the man had been healed, they made it clear: 'It is Jesus' name and the faith that comes through him that has given this complete healing to him, as you can all see' (Acts 3:16).

Later when hauled before the Jewish Council they repeated this assertion: 'It is by the name of Jesus Christ of Nazareth . . . that this man stands before you completely healed' (Acts 4:10).

The name of Jesus has lost none of its significance, meaning, power or authority since Bible times. His name is still the name above every other name. His name is still the only name by which men can be saved. By faith in this name, the sick man can still be healed for the glory of God.

The name of Jesus can be powerful and effective in your life. You are 'surnamed' in Christ Jesus. You are told to pray in His name and that everything you do and say is to be in His name. 'And whatever you do, whether in word or deed, do it all in the name of the Lord Jesus, giving thanks to God the Father through him' (Col. 3:17).

Understand, therefore, the enormous privilege God gives you when inviting you to pray in His name. Imagine what could happen in your experience as you begin to speak and act in His name. See what you could accomplish as you obey God's command to heal the sick, because by faith in the name of Jesus people are healed today.

Hear His words of promise to you. Let these words sink into your heart. Jesus speaks them to you!

---

**Meditation:**
I WILL DO WHATEVER YOU ASK IN MY NAME (JOHN 14:13).

And everyone who calls on the name of the Lord will be saved (ACTS 2:21).

In the name of Jesus Christ of Nazareth, walk (ACTS 3:6).

**Praise:**
Ascribe to the Lord the glory due to his name (PS. 29:2).

# 70. I Strengthen You

'The Lord gives strength to his people; the Lord blesses His people with peace' (PS. 29:11).

Thank you, Lord, that you promise to strengthen me.

**READING:** ISAIAH 41:9–13

I took you from the ends of the earth, from its farthest corners I called you. I said, 'You are my servant'; I have chosen you and not rejected you. So do not fear for I am with you; do not be dismayed, for I am your God. I will strengthen you and help you; I will uphold you with my righteous right hand. 'All who rage against you will surely be ashamed and disgraced; those who oppose you will be as nothing and perish. Though you search for your enemies, you will not find them. Those who wage war against you will be as nothing at all. For I am the Lord, your God, who takes hold of your right hand and says to you, Do not fear; I will help you.'

---

The Lord is the strength of your life. There will be many occasions when you will feel weak and useless, totally inadequate, a failure even. It will seem that the Lord will reach deep within you to expose your insecurities. Then He will show you His love. Yes, His love is for the real you, not some projection of yourself that you want others to believe in.

It is *you* He has called and chosen, *you* He has made acceptable, *you* in whom He lives by the power of His Holy Spirit. It is you to whom He has given a new life.

You do not have to be bound by your past, by your sins, failure and inadequacy. Yet the Lord can work through your weakness in His strength. This was the lesson Paul learned well. 'My grace is sufficient for you, for my power is made perfect in weakness' (2 Cor. 12:9). This does not mean that

God's power is ever imperfect, but that the complete scope of His power can be manifested through your weakness. He has chosen 'the weak things of the world to shame the strong' (1 Cor. 1:27).

Again and again the Lord tells us not to fear, because He knows that often this will be our natural reaction; 'I have chosen you and have not rejected you. So do not fear for I am with you; do not be dismayed, for I am your God. I will strengthen you and help you; I will uphold you with my righteous right hand' (Isa. 41:9–10).

So you can learn to stand firm in the knowledge of what you mean to Him and what He has done for you. You can give yourself to Him knowing He will use you and work through you despite all your inadequacies. 'Therefore, my dear brothers, stand firm. Let nothing move you. Always give yourselves fully to the work of the Lord, because you know that your labour in the Lord is not in vain' (1 Cor. 15:58).

Again Paul urges: 'Be on your guard; stand firm in the faith; be men of courage; be strong. Do everything in love' (1 Cor. 16:13–14). Stand firm in the faith of who you are in Christ. Be bold in your faith, for you know the Lord will not fail you when you put your trust in Him. You may feel very weak, but He will not allow you to fall or be overcome by events as you look to Him. Be strong, not only by your own efforts, but by resting in His strength.

When you feel a failure in your inability to love, know that the Holy Spirit has given you all the resources of His love. When you sense you have such little power, know His almighty power can flow through your weakness.

'It is for freedom that Christ has set us free. Stand firm, then, and do not let yourselves be burdened again by a yoke of slavery' (Gal. 5:1). Stand firm against all the devices of the enemy who wants you to believe that you are a useless failure.

You are God's child, loved and appreciated by Him. He watches over you and strengthens you in your weakness. He speaks into your areas of insecurity to free you from them and to teach you that He is more than adequate for your every need. He has accepted *you* and loves *you*.

**Meditation:**
I AM WITH YOU . . . I WILL STRENGTHEN
YOU AND HELP YOU (ISA. 41:10).

My grace is sufficient for you, for my power is made
perfect in weakness (2 COR. 12:9).

God chose the weak things of the world to shame the
strong (1 COR. 1:27).

**Praise:**
The Lord is my strength and my song (PS. 118:14).

# 71. *Always Giving Thanks*

'Be joyful always; pray continually; give thanks in all circumstances, for this is God's will for you in Christ Jesus'
(1 THESS. 5:16–18).

Father, I want to be thankful in every situation and so fulfil
your purpose for me.

**READING:** PSALM 30:11–12
You turned my wailing into dancing; you removed
my sackcloth and clothed me with joy, that my heart
may sing to you and not be silent. O Lord my God, I
will give you thanks for ever.

One of the most destructive things in the Christian life is
self-pity. When our difficulties are compared to those of Paul,
for example, we have hardly any right to call them problems!
Yet, he rejoiced no matter what his circumstances. He wrote
to the Philippians from prison telling them to rejoice in the
Lord always. When thrown into prison Peter sang hymns! As

he praised God the doors were flung open! Praise releases the supernatural power of God into the situation.

Turning the direction of our hearts and minds to the Lord with joy and thanksgiving is no flippant gesture. It is not a matter of saying, 'Praise the Lord, anyway!' We learn to be grateful that in every situation the Lord is present with us, ready to help and encourage, to forgive and to heal, to enable and guide us.

When wanting to encourage others it's not a question of slapping them on the back and saying; 'Well, you have a lot for which to be thankful!' True as that is, we have to learn to, 'Rejoice with those who rejoice; mourn with those who mourn' (Rom. 12:15). Sensitively you can try to identify with the person you want to help and understand his position. Then you can direct his attention to the Lord, to His love and provision showing him why he can be thankful:

Thankful that He is with them;
Thankful that He never fails;
Thankful that He is faithful;
Thankful that He reigns in victory;
Thankful that He understands us because He has shared our humanity;
Thankful that His love and power is more than sufficient for every situation.

But remember, much harm can be done by giving the right answer in the wrong way. There are times when you cannot know another's grief, even if you may have experienced something similar yourself. What matters is that you are there, able to express God's love to the person, to show His mercy and compassion. In that way the person in grief can identify with you and when that identification has taken place, you can begin to turn that person's eyes in the right direction. You can start lovingly to thank the Lord, even in that situation. There have been many times when I have been amazed at the effect of thanksgiving on someone in deep distress. When praying with them I have simply begun to thank the Lord and before long the needy one is beginning to view his or her circumstances with an entirely new perspective.

The whole world can so easily seem distorted by what is going on within us. This is why we need to help one another to focus on the Lord. My moods, feelings and situations may change, but He is the great unchanging one. He is the solid rock on which my life is built. If my trust is in Him, the Lord will see me through. He even promises: 'I have made you and I will carry you; I will sustain you and I will rescue you' (Isa. 46:4).

When you are unable to walk through a situation, He will even carry you! He knows when you need to be carried and when you are to walk on your own two feet, without adopting a self-reliant attitude that says, 'I'll get there by myself!'

At times when it is difficult to pray, let alone praise God, the gift of speaking in tongues can be an immense help. 'He who speaks in a tongue edifies himself' (1 Cor. 14:4). The Spirit within you can always pray, and He knows exactly what to say! The Spirit ministers to you as you pray in tongues. Gradually your spirit is lifted and you are aware that God has replaced the heaviness with praise and thanksgiving for Him. He is the Lord who turns your wailing into dancing, who clothes you with joy.

Again and again the Spirit will want to encourage you to rejoice in the Lord and to give Him thanks. Hear Him now and set your heart and mind on putting this word into operation in your life every day.

---

**Meditation:**
GIVE THANKS IN ALL CIRCUMSTANCES (1 THESS. 5:18).

I have made you and I will carry you (IS A. 46:4).

Rejoice in the Lord always . . . Rejoice! (PHIL. 4:4).

**Praise:**
In God we make our boast all day long, and we will praise your name for ever (PS. 44:8).

# PART EIGHT

# YOUR LIFE IN HOLINESS AND GLORY

# 72. I am Holy

'For he chose us in him before the creation of the world to be holy and blameless in his sight' (EPH. 1:4).

You alone can make me holy, O Lord.

**READING:** REVELATION 4:8–11
Each of the four living creatures had six wings and was covered with eyes all around, even under his wings. Day and night they never stop saying: 'Holy, holy, holy is the Lord God Almighty, who was, and is, and is to come.' Whenever the living creatures give glory, honour and thanks to him who sits on the throne and who lives for ever and ever, the twenty-four elders fall down before him who sits on the throne, and worship him who lives for ever and ever. They lay their crowns before the throne and say: 'You are worthy, our Lord and God, to receive glory and honour and power, for you created all things, and by your will they were created and have their being.'

---

God's essential nature is to be holy. It is impossible to describe adequately what this means, for the Lord in the essential nature of His being, is beyond description. We can say He is whole, complete and perfect in Himself; but this is a very inadequate definition of His holiness. He is above and beyond all He has made, and above anything we can conceive. 'I am the Lord, your Holy One' (Isa. 43:15).

What does a holy God want with us who are obviously so unholy in ourselves? To make us holy and fit to reign with Him in His holy heaven.

The heavenly host is holy, but even the creatures, elders and angels who surround God's throne bow before Him as they sing day and night the hymn which proclaims His holiness.

The holiness of God is somehow so much greater than the holiness of any He has made, in heaven or on earth.

Jesus came to make you holy, fit to come before His holy throne in worship and prayer. You can 'have confidence to enter the Most Holy Place by the blood of Jesus' (Heb. 10:19).

Paul says: 'It is God's will that you should be holy' (1 Thess. 4:3). But the very word 'holiness' sends a shiver down the spine of many Christians. They immediately think of legalistic holiness movements in which there is little joy or power. Or they imagine holiness is something beyond them, for great spiritual 'saints'. Yet, according to the New Testament, every Christian is a saint, one who is set apart for God and called to be holy.

You are not a Christian unless you are a saint! And here is the secret of living in holiness. This is not a goal that you will inevitably fail to attain. It is the essential nature of God's own Spirit who lives within you. He is the *Holy* Spirit. To live a holy life is to follow the leading of the Holy Spirit and obey the Lord. He will never lead you into unholiness or what God considers unrighteous.

The Holy Spirit does more than show you what to do; He enables you to do it! He is the Spirit of holiness within you wanting to be expressed in your life.

Jesus lived the holy life here on earth. To be holy in practical ways is to be like Him. You need to have a positive view of holiness and to see that it is possible for you to live in holiness because you have the presence, the life and the power of the Holy One within you. To be holy is to be full of love, full of joy, full of peace and power and forgiveness, full of the fruit of the Holy Spirit.

The words of this meditation are not only a command; they are a promise. There may be many ways in which you fail to be like Jesus; but He is at work in you changing you into His likeness from one degree of glory to another. Do not be discouraged. Know that the Lord will complete the work He has begun in you. 'May God himself, the God of peace, sanctify you through and through. May your whole spirit, soul and body be kept blameless at the coming of our Lord

Jesus Christ. The one who calls you is faithful and he will do it' (1 Thess. 5:23–4).

Above all remember the revelation of God's Word; you are already made holy in Christ, sanctified in Him (1 Cor. 1:30). The Lord sees this as an accomplished fact. Your holiness is not what you accomplish, but the holiness you have in Christ. His holiness has become your holiness. No wonder you are accepted by the Father. You live in the Holy One, and the Holy One lives in you!

---

**Meditation:**
BE HOLY BECAUSE I, THE LORD YOUR GOD, AM HOLY (LEV. 19:2).

It is God's will that you should be holy (1 THESS. 4:3).

[You are] sanctified in Christ Jesus and called to be holy (1 COR. 1:2).

**Praise:**
Your ways, O God, are holy. What god is so great as our God? (PS. 77:13).

# 73. I have Wisdom

'I guide you in the way of wisdom and lead you along straight paths' (PROV. 4:11).

Father, I ask for wisdom and believe you give this to me by your Holy Spirit.

**READING:** 1 CORINTHIANS 1:25–31
For the foolishness of God is wiser than man's wisdom, and the weakness of God is stronger than man's strength.
Brothers, think of what you were when you were called. Not many of you were wise by human standards; not many were influential; not many were of noble birth. But God chose the foolish things of the world to shame the wise; God chose the weak things of the world to shame the strong. He chose the lowly things of this world and the despised things – and the things that are not – to nullify the things that are, so that no-one may boast before him. It is because of him that you are in Christ Jesus, who has become for us wisdom from God – that is, our righteousness, holiness and redemption. Therefore, as it is written: 'Let him who boasts boast in the Lord.'

---

The Lord is wise. Even man's greatest wisdom is only foolishness in God's sight. '"For my thoughts are not your thoughts, neither are your ways my ways," declares the Lord. "As the heavens are higher than the earth, so are my ways higher than your ways and my thoughts than your thoughts"' (Isa. 55:8–9).

Intellectual pride is one of the greatest sins in modern society, keeping many from faith and the salvation God desires to give. Those who judge God make themselves out to be greater and wiser than He. Those who humble themselves before Him not only come to know Him, but also find their thinking enlarged by God's supernatural thinking.

If you accept the Lord's words and store up His commands within you,

> turning your ear to wisdom and applying your heart to understanding, and if you call out for insight and cry aloud for understanding, and if you look for it as for silver and search for it as for hidden treasure, then you will understand the fear of the Lord and find the knowledge of God. For the Lord gives wisdom, and from his mouth come knowledge and understanding (Prov. 2:2–6).

To be wise with God's wisdom is to be wise indeed. To be wise in the world's eyes is mere foolishness before God. And He is always willing to give you His wisdom when you acknowledge your need of it. James says that, 'If any of you lacks wisdom, he should ask God, who gives generously to all without finding fault, and it will be given to him' (Jas. 1:5). However, the one who asks must believe and not doubt when he asks. James later describes the nature of this wisdom. 'But the wisdom that comes from heaven is first of all pure; then peace-loving, considerate, submissive, full of mercy and good fruit, impartial and sincere' (Jas. 3:17).

The Holy Spirit is the Spirit of wisdom and the means by which God imparts His wisdom to us. Those who set their minds in opposition to God's truth display their foolishness. Who is wiser than God? Who has more knowledge than His Son?

Often God chooses those who seem of little consequence in worldly terms, in order that He might work through them in His sovereign power. Then it is clearly seen that what is accomplished is not man's work, but God working through man.

Jesus is wisdom personified, our wisdom from God. The wisdom of God is seen in His life and ministry and the Holy Spirit wants to produce those same qualities in us. James describes these as purity, peace, love, consideration, submission, mercy, faithfulness, impartiality and sincerity. It is wise to live in purity; impurity leads to a sense of guilt and shame and makes it impossible to have confidence before the Holy God. It is wise to be at peace; not to be anxious and fretful, not to be at odds with others. It is wise to love; for only then can you reflect the Lord's love and receive all He wants to give you. It is wise to be considerate towards others. It is wise to be submissive, for God does not walk with the proud: He dwells with the humble of heart. It is wise to be merciful, for then you shall obtain mercy, the mercies of God that are new for you every morning.

It is wise to be faithful for then you can inherit the promises of God, knowing His faithfulness towards you. It is wise to be impartial and to seek to live in peace with all men. It is wise to be sincere, for God hates hypocrisy and insincerity, for He is truth.

These are the practical outworkings of God's holiness and righteousness in your life. Because Jesus is wisdom from God for us, He is our righteousness, holiness and redemption, Paul says. We realise we can produce nothing of lasting value in ourselves; our total dependence is therefore on the Lord to work in us and through us.

'I am the Lord your God, who teaches you what is best for you, who directs you in the way you should go. If only you had paid attention to my commands, your peace would have been like a river, your righteousness like the waves of the sea' (Isa. 48:17–18).

The wisdom of God brings true counsel and insight as well as understanding and power into your daily life. When perplexed, the Holy Spirit is willing to speak a word of wisdom to you. When you ask for wisdom, God is ready to give it to you. He wants you to understand things from His perspective so that you come to the right decisions that are pleasing to Him.

Sometimes we opt for the foolishness of sin. But the Lord with His constant patience brings us back to a realisation that it is always wiser to walk in His ways, and receive the riches that are the benefit of His wisdom.

**Meditation:**
COUNSEL AND SOUND JUDGMENT ARE
MINE; I HAVE UNDERSTANDING AND
POWER (PROV. 8:14).

I am the Lord your God, who teaches you what is best
for you (ISA. 48:17).

For the Lord gives wisdom, and from his mouth come
knowledge and understanding (PROV. 2:6).

**Praise:**
I will praise the Lord, who counsels me (PS. 16:7).

# 74. *Walking as Jesus Did*

'Whoever claims to live in him must walk as Jesus did' (1 JOHN
2:6).

Holy Spirit, please help me to walk as Jesus did.

**READING:** 1 PETER 1:13–23
Therefore, prepare your minds for action; be self-
controlled; set your hope fully on the grace to be given
you when Jesus Christ is revealed. As obedient children, do not conform to the evil desires you had when
you lived in ignorance. But just as he who called you is
holy, so be holy in all you do; for it is written: 'Be holy,
because I am holy.'

Since you call on a Father who judges each man's
work impartially, live your lives as strangers here in
reverent fear. For you know that it was not with
perishable things such as silver or gold that you were
redeemed from the empty way of life handed down to

you from your forefathers, but with the precious blood of Christ, a lamb without blemish or defect. He was chosen before the creation of the world, but was revealed in these last times for your sake. Through him you believe in God, who raised him from the dead and glorified him, and so your faith and hope are in God.

Now that you have purified yourselves by obeying the truth so that you have sincere love for your brothers, love one another deeply, from the heart. For you have been born again, not of perishable seed, but of imperishable, through the living and enduring word of God.

---

Jesus was tempted in every way as we are, yet never sinned. Paul tells us: 'No temptation has seized you except what is common to man. And God is faithful; he will not let you be tempted beyond what you can bear. But when you are tempted, he will also provide a way out so that you can stand up under it' (1 Cor. 10:13).

The Holy Spirit working within us, encourages us to refuse temptation. There is no sin in being tempted, only in yielding to the temptation. John says we are to walk as Jesus did. At first this seems like an impossible ideal because we know of His sinless character. At the same time we also recognise our own proneness to yield to temptation and so fail to walk as Jesus did.

The Holy Spirit helps you do what Jesus would do in your position. There is no need to fear holiness. This is God expressing His life through your imperfect life. Be thankful for the ways in which this already happens. If you recognise there are things in your life that are opposed to His purposes, ask the Lord to forgive you, and call upon the Holy Spirit to help you.

There is a right kind of fear of God, when we are in awe of Him and do not desire in any way to displease Him. Peter says that you purify yourself by obeying the truth. We have peace with God when we know our hearts are pure before Him and that we desire only what He wants. 'Who may ascend the hill of the Lord? Who may stand in his holy place? He who has clean hands and a pure heart' (Ps. 24:3–4).

Such purity of heart is expressed in true, selfless love for the brethren; love that is deep and comes from the heart. Every one of Jesus's actions was motivated by such love, first for His Father and then for those to whom He ministered.

God continues the process of refining your heart, showing you the hidden faults. Do not be discouraged when He does this; it is part of the way in which He expresses His love for you. Peter later says; 'Dear friends, I urge you, as aliens and strangers in the world, to abstain from sinful desires, which war against your soul. Live such good lives among the pagans that, though they accuse you of doing wrong, they may see your good deeds and glorify God on the day he visits us' (1 Pet. 2:11–12).

When you agree to do what Jesus would do you know you bring glory to the Father. If you decide to do anything He would not do, this will cause grief both to Him and yourself. There is peace in walking as Jesus did; only confusion and upset if you choose your own path instead. 'He himself bore our sins in his body on the tree, so that we might die to sins and live for righteousness' (1 Pet. 2:24).

God always has your best interests at heart. He knows how you will benefit by walking in righteousness and truth, conquering temptation and expressing His love. 'Finally, all of you, live in harmony with one another; be sympathetic, love as brothers, be compassionate and humble. Do not repay evil with evil or insult with insult, but with blessing, because to this you were called so that you may inherit a blessing' (1 Pet. 3:8–9).

---

**Meditation:**
WHOEVER CLAIMS TO LIVE IN HIM MUST WALK AS JESUS DID (1 JOHN 2:6).

For he chose us in him . . . to be holy and blameless in his sight (EPH. 1:4).

God disciplines us for our good, that we may share in his holiness (HEB. 12:10).


**Praise:**
Show me your ways, O Lord, teach me your paths (PS. 25:4).


# 75. *The Open Door*

'See, I have placed before you an open door that no-one can shut' (REV. 3:8).

Lord, draw me into your holy presence, please.


**READING:** REVELATION 4:1–2
After this I looked, and there before me was a door standing open in heaven. And the voice I had first heard speaking to me like a trumpet said, 'Come up here, and I will show you what must take place after this.' At once I was in the Spirit, and there before me was a throne in heaven with someone sitting on it.

---

God is holy. Heaven is the dwelling-place of His holy presence. The hymn the heavenly host sings day and night is: 'Holy, holy, holy is the Lord God Almighty, who was, and is, and is to come' (Rev. 4:8).

And yet it is into this holy place that the Lord welcomes you. Jesus has gone to prepare a place for you; today and every day He calls you into the holy of holies to enjoy fellowship with you.

It seems inexplicable that the holy God should delight in fellowship with us. It is the overwhelming evidence of His love that He should send His Son to endure suffering and death to make this possible.

How it must grieve the Lord, therefore, when we pray from a distance without drawing near. He has set an open door before you. Because He has opened it, no one can shut it. This is the door into His glory and He encourages you to walk through it.

It is not surprising that you hesitate at first. It seems inconceivable that we could be worthy enough to go through this doorway into the holy presence of the Lord and enjoy His glory. Of yourself you could never be worthy of such a privilege. However, Jesus has made you worthy. When you are cleansed from your sins you are made righteous in His sight. And you live in Christ Jesus. Because you are in Him you belong to the glory: 'And God raised us up with Christ and seated us with him in the heavenly realms in Christ Jesus' (Eph. 2:6).

The secret to going through that open door is knowing you are able to do so. Many Christians worship the Lord faithfully without ever realising they have such a privilege.

Imagine you are in a large room. Along one wall is a doorway with the door thrown open. Through the opening, shafts of light stream into the room. You are in the room next to the glory. Hear the Lord say to you, as He said to John: 'Come up here, and I will show you what must take place after this' (Rev. 4:1).

Perhaps you have often asked the Lord to come to you. Now He is asking you to come to Him. Such an invitation can hardly be refused. Why do you hesitate? Is it because you realise that certain things in your life are not holy and do not belong in the glory? Would you be ashamed to come before God's very throne in such a state?

Very well, then, leave behind in the room next to the glory these things which do not belong to the glory. Spend time throwing off 'everything that hinders and the sin that so easily entangles' (Heb. 12:1). Ask Jesus to forgive the sins, all the things of which you are ashamed, those things about you that are not like Him and cannot reflect His glory.

Take off the burdens, those things that cause anxiety and

fear. Be sure you forgive any who have hurt you in any way. Hold nothing back from Him who sees all. Be humble and honest with Him.

Know that Jesus is saying to you, 'your sins are forgiven' (Mark 2:5). This means He has freed you from everything that could deter you from passing through the open doorway.

Use your imagination to picture the scene. See yourself approaching the doorway. The streams of God's glory fall upon you and you hear His voice, 'Come up here.' He is waiting for you; He is ready to welcome you.

You pass through the doorway. There before you is a throne, immense in size; and on it Someone is sitting, the King of Glory. He is surrounded by His heavenly hosts bowing before Him in worship. Join them; worship the King from your heart.

See His hands extended to you in love. Then see the marks of the cross, the cost of bringing you into this holy place. Hear His words of assurance; He loves you, accepts you, wants you to reign with Him eternally.

Perhaps you will see Him lift you into His arms. Perhaps you will hear a word spoken to your heart, a word of encouragement or correction as He reveals His purpose to you. Perhaps you will understand He is asking what you want Him to do for you. Answer Him, with the boldness of faith that comes with knowing you have access to the throne. He may give you a commission, something He is sending you to do in His name.

Every time I pass through this doorway, the experience is different. However, you are not seeking experiences, but to draw near to the holy Lord, who is your God and Father.

---

**Meditation:**
COME UP HERE, AND I WILL SHOW YOU
WHAT MUST TAKE PLACE AFTER THIS
(REV. 4:1).

See, I have placed before you an open door that no-one can shut (REV. 3:8).

Holy, holy, holy is the Lord God Almighty, who was, and is, and is to come (REV. 4:8).

**Praise:**
Holy, holy, holy is the Lord God Almighty; the whole earth is full of His glory (ISA. 6:3).

# 76. Confidence before God

'I tell you the truth, whoever hears my word and believes him who sent me has eternal life and will not be condemned; he has crossed over from death to life' (JOHN 5:24).

Lord Jesus, may I always have the confidence to know you hear me and answer me when I pray.

**READING: 1 JOHN 3:21–4**
Dear friends, if our hearts do not condemn us, we have confidence before God and receive from him anything we ask, because we obey his commands and do what pleases him. And this is his command: to believe in the name of his Son, Jesus Christ, and to love one another as he commanded us. Those who obey his commands live in him, and he in them. And this is how we know that he lives in us: We know it by the Spirit he gave us.

Without condemnation we can have confidence before God, 'we have confidence to enter the Most Holy Place by the blood of Jesus, by a new and living way opened for us through the curtain, that is, his body' (Heb. 10:19–20).

The blood of Jesus has freed you from all condemnation and has opened the way for you into the Lord's Holy Presence. You can stand before His throne, clothed in the righteousness of Jesus, knowing the Father loves you and accepts you and wants to meet you in your need.

John heard Jesus give His wonderful prayer promises. About fifty years later he wrote his first Epistle. Those were fifty years of Spirit-filled ministry in which he had ample opportunity to test those promises in practice. He discovered they were true within the context in which Jesus gave them: 'If you remain in me and my words remain in you, ask whatever you wish, and it will be given you' (John 15:7).

If you continue in Jesus and allow His words to live in you, your heart will not be condemned and you will have confidence before God that He will answer your prayer. This does not mean you have to attain a certain degree of sanctity before God will listen to you. He hears the cry from the heart of every one of His children. It does mean He wants you to walk in faithful obedience to the Word He sets before you.

John discovered that we receive whatever we ask because:

1. *Our hearts do not condemn us;*
2. *We obey the Lord;*
3. *We do what pleases Him – offering our hearts and lives to Him that He may have His way with us.*

To pray in the name of Jesus, is to pray as He would pray, seeing the situation from His perspective and believing God will deal with the matter. We cannot imagine Jesus praying without such faith. 'Now faith is being sure of what we hope for and certain of what we do not see' (Heb. 11:1).

If we are seeking to please the Lord, living by faith in Him, our hearts will not condemn us. We shall not always get everything right, but when we sin or fail we turn to the Lord in His mercy and graciousness and receive forgiveness – not allowing ourselves to feel condemned by the enemy, by others, or by our own sense of failure. We have confidence because we are sure of who God is, the Faithful One who is perfect love, for whom nothing is impossible; the One in whom we live, and move and have our being. It is so important to ensure you are right with God and others, that nothing may destroy your confidence in Him.

Draw right into His Holy Presence, whenever you pray. See yourself before His throne. This is where you belong. This is the place He has prepared for you. You do not have to stand far off. Because you are in Christ you can draw near with a sincere heart in full assurance of faith (Heb. 10:22). 'This is the assurance we have in approaching God: that if we ask anything according to his will, he hears us. And if we know that he hears us – whatever we ask – we know that we have what we asked of him' (1 John 5:14–15).

**Meditation:**
WE HAVE CONFIDENCE BEFORE GOD AND RECEIVE FROM HIM ANYTHING WE ASK (1 JOHN 3:21).

If we ask anything according to his will, he hears us (1 JOHN 5:14).

Such confidence as this is ours through Christ before God (2 COR. 3:4).

**Praise:**
Lift up your hands in the sanctuary and praise the Lord (PS. 134:2).

# 77. The Glory of the Lord

'To them God has chosen to make known among the Gentiles the glorious riches of this mystery, which is Christ in you, the hope of glory' (COL. 1:27).

Lord, please continue to change me from one degree of glory to another.

**READING:** REVELATION 22:1–5

Then the angel showed me the river of the water of life, as clear as crystal, flowing from the throne of God and of the Lamb down the middle of the great street of the city. On each side of the river stood the tree of life, bearing twelve crops of fruit, yielding its fruit every month. And the leaves of the tree are for the healing of the nations. No longer will there be any curse. The throne of God and of the Lamb will be in the city, and his servants will serve him. They will see his face, and his name will be on their foreheads. There will be no more night. They will not need the light of a lamp or the light of the sun, for the Lord God will give them light. And they will reign for ever and ever.

---

What is God's purpose for you? To know His glory. All have sinned and as a consequence have fallen short, or misused the glory God intended for them. That is the devastating consequence of sin; it deprives men and women of the glory for which they were created.

Praise be to God! He has provided us with a saviour – we can be cleansed of our sins and receive the revelation of God's glory. 'And we, who with unveiled faces all reflect the Lord's glory, are being transformed into his likeness with ever-increasing glory, which comes from the Lord, who is the Spirit' (2 Cor. 3:18). Jesus has removed the veil that separated man from God and now you can know His glory. Even more amazing is that God says in His Word that you 'reflect the Lord's glory'. How can such a thing be true?

Jesus prayed that the Father would glorify Him as He went obediently to the cross. The glory for us is on the other side of the cross. Once we have known the cleansing of His blood we can receive the revelation of His glory. Jesus prayed: 'I have given them the glory that you gave me, that they may be one as we are one' (John 17:22).

Jesus displayed God's glory in the things He did. 'I have brought you glory on earth by completing the work you gave me to do. And now, Father, glorify me in your presence with the glory I had with you before the world began' (John 17:4–5). As God's children we too are to show His glory in the works He performs through us. God is glorified every time a sinner turns to Him in repentance and receives salvation, every time someone is baptised in the Holy Spirit or healed. He loves to give to His children and it blesses Him to see His life expressed in their lives.

We glorify the Lord in our lives as we live by faith putting our trust in His words of promise. We glorify Him by a life of faithful obedience, being prepared to deny ourselves in order that we might follow Him. We glorify Him when we allow His love to flow through us to others. '. . . live lives worthy of God, who calls you into his kingdom and glory' (1 Thess. 2:12).

As you pray He wants to reveal His heavenly glory to you, giving you a foretaste of the awesome joys that are to come. Such times are a great blessing; you sense a release in your heart and want to express your wonder, love and praise to Him.

The Holy Spirit is leading you to a greater revelation of God's glory, to the fulfilment of His purpose. When you see Him face to face, you will be like Him, radiant in His glory. 'He called you to this through our gospel, that you might share in the glory of our Lord Jesus Christ' (2 Thess. 2:14).

You are a fellow-heir with Christ. That means you are to share the inheritance He has received. You share now in the cost of living as a child of His kingdom in the world, of being a faithful witness in the face of misunderstanding and opposition, so that you will share in the glory to come.

The Lord sees this as accomplished: 'And those he predestined, he also called; those he called, he also justified; those he justified, he also glorified' (Rom. 8:30). He sees the whole process from beginning to end. What He has begun in you He will surely bring to completion for He sees it as already completed. The work is done totally in Jesus. 'Then Jesus said, "Did I not tell you that if you believed, you would see the glory of God?"' (John 11:40).

This was Jesus's prayer for you and all who believe in Him: 'Father, I want those you have given me to be with me where I am, and to see my glory, the glory you have given me because you loved me before the creation of the world' (John 17:24).

---

**Meditation:**
I HAVE GIVEN THEM THE GLORY THAT YOU GAVE ME, THAT THEY MAY BE ONE AS WE ARE ONE (JOHN 17:22).

I am going . . . to prepare a place for you (JOHN 14:2).

I will come back and take you to be with me that you also may be where I am (JOHN 14:3).

**Praise:**
Ascribe to the Lord the glory due to his name (PS. 29:2).

# 78. Press On

'Therefore, since we are surrounded by such a great cloud of witnesses, let us throw off everything that hinders and the sin that so easily entangles, and let us run with perseverance the race marked out for us. Let us fix our eyes on Jesus, the author and perfecter of our faith' (HEB. 12:1–2).

Dear Father, please give me the grace to remain faithful to the end.

### READING: PHILIPPIANS 3:7–14
But whatever was to my profit I now consider loss for the sake of Christ. What is more, I consider everything a loss compared to the surpassing greatness of knowing Christ Jesus my Lord, for whose sake I have lost all things. I consider them rubbish, that I may gain Christ and be found in him, not having a righteousness of my own that comes from the law, but that which is through faith in Christ – the righteousness that comes from God and is by faith. I want to know Christ and the power of his resurrection and the fellowship of sharing in his sufferings, becoming like him in his death, and so, somehow, to attain to the resurrection from the dead.

Not that I have already obtained all this, or have already been made perfect, but I press on to take hold of that for which Christ Jesus took hold of me. Brothers, I do not consider myself yet to have taken hold of it. But one thing I do: Forgetting what is behind and straining towards what is ahead, I press on towards the goal to win the prize for which God has called me heavenwards in Christ Jesus.

---

Life is a matter of priorities. Every day is full of decisions. Paul counted everything else as rubbish in comparison with knowing the Lord Jesus. He never wanted to be a Christian originally, let alone an apostle; but God took hold of his life because He loved him and wanted to make him holy, like Jesus. His ministry was to be that of an apostle extending His kingdom, not persecuting the Church.

Paul knew God had taken hold of his life for a purpose and he wanted to 'press on to take hold of that for which Christ Jesus took hold of me' (Phil. 3:12). So he learned to look forward to what lay ahead. He was reaching out for the next thing that God wanted to do in his life or the next way in which He wanted to use him.

We should all do well to follow Paul's advice. Ahead of you lies a greater revelation of God's love for you than you have so far received. Ahead of you there will be more challenges to your faith, which will result in a strengthening of your trust in Jesus. Ahead of you the Father will do more pruning in your life, but you will be more fruitful as a result, and you will reflect more of His holiness and glory.

Yes, there will be difficulties and disappointments and even failure when you trust in yourself, but there will also be rich blessing and victory. The Lord in His goodness will lead you through each situation. And all the time, like Paul, you will be drawing nearer towards the goal. 'I press on towards the goal to win the prize for which God has called me heavenwards in Christ Jesus' (v.14).

Remember, 'we know that in all things God works for the good of those who love him, who have been called according to his purpose. For those God foreknew he also predestined to be conformed to the likeness of his Son, that he might be the firstborn among many brothers' (Rom. 8:28–9). How comforting to know you are in God's purpose and that He will ensure the plan for your life is fulfilled. Day by day you can co-operate with Him in this, rejoicing that He has made you His own.

Your love for Him creates in you the desire to make Him known to others, to pray for those who do not know Him: the lost, the desperate, the lonely, the depressed. You will know the need to pray for revival in the Church, that the life, love and power of Jesus might be revealed to the world through His people; to look forward to the time when there will be a great spiritual awakening in the nation and many are brought into God's kingdom.

We live, not for ourselves, but for His kingdom, to see His reign extended on earth, His will done here as in heaven. We live to make Him known, that men and women may be saved from death and brought to a saving knowledge of Jesus, being brought into His kingdom and receiving the gift of eternal life. We live to glorify the King, giving Him the praise and honour He alone deserves.

And we long for the time when the King will return in glory to claim all who belong to Him!

---

**Meditation:**
HALLELUJAH! FOR OUR LORD GOD ALMIGHTY REIGNS (REV. 19:6).

Whoever is thirsty let him come; and whoever wishes, let him take the free gift of the water of life (REV. 22:17).

Amen. Come, Lord Jesus (REV. 22:20).

**Praise:**
The Lord Almighty is with us; the God of Jacob is our fortress (PS. 46:7).